Expanding College Access
for Urban Youth

Expanding College Access for Urban Youth

What Schools and Colleges Can Do

Edited by

Tyrone C. Howard
Jonli D. Tunstall
Terry K. Flennaugh

TEACHERS COLLEGE PRESS

TEACHERS COLLEGE | COLUMBIA UNIVERSITY
NEW YORK AND LONDON

Published by Teachers College Press, 1234 Amsterdam Avenue, New York, NY 10027

Cover design and illustration by Emmanuel Freeman.

Library of Congress Cataloging-in-Publication Data

Names: Howard, Tyrone C. (Tyrone Caldwell), editor.
Title: Expanding college access for urban youth : what schools and colleges can do / edited by Tyrone C. Howard, Jonli Tunstall, Terry K. Flennaugh,.
Description: New York, NY : Teachers College Press, [2016] | Includes bibliographical references and index.
Identifiers: LCCN 2016003517| ISBN 9780807757642 (pbk. : alk. paper) | ISBN 9780807757659 (hardcover : alk. paper)
Subjects: LCSH: Urban youth—Education (Higher)—United States. | Universities and colleges—United States—Admission. | Educational equalization—United States.
Classification: LCC LC5141 .E86 2016 | DDC 378.0086/94—dc23
LC record available at http://lccn.loc.gov/2016003517

ISBN 978-0-8077-5764-2 (paper)
ISBN 978-0-8077-5765-9 (hardcover)
ISBN 978-0-8077-7476-2 (ebook)

Printed on acid-free paper
Manufactured in the United States of America

23 22 21 20 19 18 17 16   8 7 6 5 4 3 2 1

Contents

One

Creating Postsecondary Access and Opportunity for Urban Youth

Terry K. Flennaugh and Tyrone C. Howard

Access to education has been a ringing hallmark of the "American narrative" almost since the nation's inception. The United States has always touted education as a fundamental commodity and unalienable right for citizens that can put them on to the pathway to upward mobility in a democratic, egalitarian, and just society (Banks, 2015). Endemic to the U.S. narrative has been the idea that educational opportunity, which is purported to be accessible to all, is an irreplaceable pillar in the pursuit of happiness, upward mobility, and self-actualization. What has often been absent from this lofty and enduring narrative is the centuries-old struggle that many groups have engaged in to ensure that they could participate in the educative process (Anderson, 1988; Carter & Wellner, 2013; Gándara, 2012; Spring, 2010; Walker, 1996). Women, indigenous peoples, enslaved Africans, colonized populations, and newly arrived immigrants have all waged contentious battles for educational access and equality for the better part of 4 centuries (Griffin, 2012). These struggles have been intense and, despite progress, fraught with setbacks, legal obstacles, and incessant racism and sexism that continue in the present day. These challenges remain ongoing because the idea that education is essential to self-empowerment, self-actualization, and transformation remains as prevalent today as it was 200 years ago.

Over the course of time, as access to pre-K–12 schooling has improved, what has become even more valued in the United States is access to postsecondary education (Shapiro et al., 2014). Postsecondary education has been viewed as an escalator mechanism of sorts, wherein individuals who attain higher levels of education have increased incomes over time, an improved quality of life, and greater access to educational and medical services (Baum, Ma, & Payea, 2013). According to Kena and colleagues (2014), American postsecondary institutions will enroll nearly 20 million students by 2022. As the number of enrollees has increased, historically marginalized groups have witnessed their numbers grow also. Data from the American Council on Education reported that college enrollment rates for African Americans, Latinos, and Asian Americans increased significantly between 1980 and 2000. African American and Latino students merit a particular focus where access and success to postsecondary education is concerned. Despite the increase over the past several decades, these two groups still dramatically lag behind their Asian American and White peers in postsecondary enrollment (Lumina Foundation, 2015a, 2015b). Although issues tied to the educational opportunities of Native American students are equally distressing and merit new approaches, that particular group will not be the focus here. While the gap between Blacks and Latinos in the pursuit of college has dwindled over the years, chronic disparities remain. In short, Blacks and Latinos lose ground at every step of the educational pipeline compared with their White and many of their Asian American peers (Howard, 2010). They are less likely to finish high school, less likely to attend college, and less likely to graduate when they get there (Aud, Fox, & KewalRamani, 2010). These facts are more disconcerting given that these groups (Latinos in particular) will continue to make up a larger part of the U.S. student and general population in the years to come. Hence the need to adequately educate these groups has major implications for economic, political, and national security factors.

What remains clear in the 2nd decade of the 21st century is that the same battles that endured for centuries around equity in and access to basic education for all groups remains entrenched in the pursuit for postsecondary education. Approximately 40% of Whites between the ages of 25 and 29 had a bachelor's degree or more and 58% of Asians held a college degree compared with only 20% of Blacks and 15% of Latinos in 2013 (Kena et al., 2014). According to Department of Education data, approximately 58% of Whites and 69% of Asians who entered 4-year colleges in 1996 had a bachelor's degree 6 years later, compared with 39% of Blacks and 46% of Latinos (Aud et al., 2012). Just under a decade later, Whites and Latinos had made nominal progress and Blacks hardly any at all. Of students who entered college in 2005, data from the National Center for Education Statistics (2012b) indicate that 62% of Whites received a degree within 6 years, versus 40% of Blacks and 51% of Latinos. Much of the gap that exists between Black and Latino students is a result of many factors at the pre-K–12 level. Research has informed us that Black and Latino students are more likely to have inexperienced and underqualified teachers (Darling Hammond, 2010), are less likely to be recommended for gifted and talented and highly rigorous courses (Advanced Placement [AP] and honors) in high school, and are more likely not to be given access to college preparatory courses despite showing high potential for success in these courses (Ford, 2013). African American and Latino students with high academic potential (as measured by PSAT scores, which have been found to correlate strongly with success in particular AP courses) are significantly less likely than their Asian and White counterparts to be enrolled in AP classes. Of students who graduated in 2011, only 20% of Black and 30% of Latino students took an AP exam for which they had potential, compared with 38% and 58% of their White and Asian peers, respectively (College Board, 2012).

There has been considerable discussion about why such an "AP-potential gap"—the difference between the number of students with potential to succeed in AP and the number who actually participate—exists and what the racial implications are. For individual students and their parents it matters for college admission, cost, and success. AP or other advanced courses are often a de facto admission requirement to selective universities, with many universities giving added weight to students who take AP courses or receive a passing score on an AP exam (Geiser & Santelices, 2004; Klopfenstein & Thomas, 2009). Colleges may grant students college credit for AP coursework, which can lower the total cost of college as well as students' time to degree completion (College Board, 2012). Further, strong AP exam scores can qualify students for scholarships and financial aid (Iatarola, Conger, & Long, 2011).

As demographics have shifted, the need to increase the educational attainment of Black and Latino groups has grown increasingly important. But an important question remains: What roles have public institutions (namely pre-K–12 and postsecondary) played in helping to ameliorate the chronic underperformance that has been a staple in many low-income, urban communities? This book does not lament the problem. To the contrary, this work centers on a school–university partnership that addresses the leaky parts of the educational pipeline in a manner that improves educational prospects, life chances, and community vitality for underserved students.

To address persistent inequities, the opening chapter of this book will explore the necessity of university–high school partnerships in providing college access work for youth of color, and in particular those in urban settings, where communities of color are higher in representation. To be clear, this work is primarily centered on African American and Latino students given their status as the nation's two largest non-White groups and the ongoing educational discrepancies that severely affect these two groups. In this chapter, and in the rest of this book, we will lay out a rationale for the need to address educational equity and viable options for low-income youth of color where postsecondary education is concerned. There will be four key areas of focus in this chapter. From the outset, we discuss the state of affairs for the nation's urban youth; the picture is encouraging in many instances yet disturbing on other fronts. In the second section of this chapter we will discuss the increasing salience of postsecondary education in the 21st century. We then provide a snapshot of urban youth in postsecondary institutions across the nation. We conclude the chapter by identifying chronic obstacles to pathways for urban youth. One prominent example is California's 1996 anti–affirmative action law, Proposition 209, with its impact on diversity in higher education, which has severely reduced possibilities for low-income youth of color. In 1996, following years of controversy over affirmative action that dated back to the 1978 U.S. Supreme Court *Bakke* decision, California became the first state to enact a formal ban on racial and other preferences, when voters approved Proposition 209. Since then, Michigan and six other states—Washington, Florida, Nebraska, Arizona, New Hampshire, and Oklahoma—have enacted similar bans. Most of these measures include language similar or identical to Prop 209's key provision: that the state (including but not limited to public colleges and universities) "shall not discriminate against, or grant preferential treatment to, any individual or group on the basis of race, sex, color, ethnicity, or national origin in the operation of public employment, public education, or public contracting."

However, among the four major ethnic/racial groups in California, African Americans still experience significant opportunity gaps where education is concerned and have not reached pre-209 levels 20 years after the proposition's introduction to the state. Consider that 23% of working-age African American adults in California have a bachelor's degree or higher compared with 42% of White adults. Moreover, African Americans are the most likely to have attended some college but then left without earning a degree, and this is most acute at the community college level, where most African American high school graduates pursue postsecondary education (Lumina Foundation, 2015a). Following rulings such as Proposition 209, there have been creative ways that universities, pre-K–12 schools, and community-based organizations have played roles in helping to disrupt some of the disturbing trends.

STATE OF AFFAIRS FOR URBAN YOUTH IN THE UNITED STATES

Many of the challenges facing students of color in the United States are tied to historical, social, and economic factors that continue to plague these groups to this day. One of the biggest factors in chronic underachievement in the

United States is poverty, particularly as it affects children. The National Child Poverty Center reports that the number of children living in deep poverty (below 50% of the poverty line) is on the rise, and schools must be equipped to respond to the challenges (Ekono, Jiang, & Smith, 2016). While poverty has affected children and families across all racial and ethnic lines, it is noteworthy that race and poverty continue to intersect in disturbing ways; schools must be prepared to respond to this reality (Anyon, 2014; Cass, 2010; Gorski, 2013). African American, Latino, Native American, and Southeast Asian students continue to be disproportionately poor, and they are twice as likely as White and Asian American students to live in poverty (U.S. Census Bureau, 2014). Needless to say, where poverty is endemic issues of race and ethnicity are not too far away (Milner, 2015). Analyzing the race-poverty nexus is essential, because there is a clear manner in which children and families of color feel the effects of poverty in a much more pervasive way compared with their White counterparts. As a common saying goes, where race, ethnicity, and poverty are concerned, "when economic woes hit, Whites get a cold, while people of color get the flu." In other words, the effects of financial distress typically have a much greater impact on families of color because these families tend to have greater job instability, less accumulated wealth, and less access to resources in times of need. U.S. Census data reveal that approximately 34.5% of Black children and 28.6% of Latino students live in poverty (U.S. Census Bureau, 2013). Urban and rural schools continue to serve students who have one or both parents unemployed, and students coming from immigrant families continue to be disproportionately poor. Moreover, according to the National Center on Poverty, the working-poor population is growing. Families that have multiple wage earners yet still live at or near the poverty level (U.S. Census Bureau, 2014) are frequently not part of the discourse on impoverished families, and this absence contributes to a strong deficit sentiment about families that can easily permeate school ideologies and practices (Milner, 2013). Cases of the working poor are key because it is important to disrupt the narrative that frames people living in poverty as lazy, unwilling to work, and in constant pursuit of government assistance or other types of handouts (Lee & Bowen, 2006).

Given this state of affairs for urban youth, schooling has been looked to as one of the primary vehicles to lift these families and communities out of poverty. Notable progress has been made in the academic performance of Black and Latino youth in U.S. schools. According to the Aud and colleagues (2013), Black and Latino youth scored higher on mathematics and reading assessments in 2012 than in 1990. Additionally, the percentage of Black and Latino youth enrolled in prekindergarten or preschool programs was higher in 2013 than in 1995. And even though Black and Latino youth attend preschools at rate higher than that of their White counterparts, they still enter elementary school academically behind (Howard, 2010). Once this gap is in place, it has proved difficult to eradicate. This is evidenced by analysis of 3rd-grade reading proficiency, in which a more concerning picture emerges for urban youth of color; African American and Latino youth make up only 18% of students who read at grade level, with similar numbers in mathematics proficiency (Aud et al., 2010). At the secondary level, Black and Latino youth remain severely underenrolled in AP and honors courses, which are vitally important for college admission, especially to the nation's more selective institutions. The academic disparities are daunting, but the data on student behavior have proved to be equally concerning where urban youth are concerned. For example, the manner in which students of color are suspended and expelled from schools is alarming. In fact, a 2014 report from the U.S. Department of Education Office for Civil Rights highlights that students of color suffer from disproportionately high suspension and expulsion rates as early as preschool. For example, African American children represented 18% of preschool enrollment but 48% of preschool children receiving more than one out-of-school suspension during the 2011–2012 academic year.

Increasing amounts of data that shed light on the schooling experiences of urban youth of color highlight how these students are woefully underprepared to pursue pathways to postsecondary colleges and universities (Jayakumar, Garces, & Fernandez, 2015). The pipeline implications for Black youth who overwhelmingly attend lower-performing elementary through high schools is characterized by lower-than-average test scores, inexperienced teachers, lower levels of resources and funding, and insufficient counselors. As a result, Black and Latino high school students are less likely than students from most other racial/ethnic groups to graduate from high school and to do so having completed the sequence of A-G coursework (series of courses in seven subject areas necessary for Cal State and University of California eligibility) that makes them eligible to apply to California's public 4-year universities.

Much of the reason for this difficulty is tied to the role that various institutions, namely home, pre-K–12 schools, and colleges and universities have had in preparing youth for postsecondary opportunities. However, the focus of this work will be primarily centered on the link between pre-K–12 schools and postsecondary institutions. We acknowledge the vital role that homes, families, parents, and communities play in the pursuit of educational excellence. There is a litany of data that speaks to this link (Lareau, 1994, 2000; Reynolds, 2010). However, given the limited influence that schools and universities have on these entities, we choose to focus on the spaces and stakeholders that have larger degrees of influence on the postsecondary matriculation of urban youth of color. The manner in which schools and communities prepare their youth for postsecondary options is crucial in light of the current demographics of the nation. The prevailing education debts (Ladson-Billings, 2006) owed by a large and growing segment of the nation's youth are concerning on multiple levels, especially when one considers the changing ethnic and racial demographics of the nation. The U.S. Department of Education released a report in February 2014 stating that for the first time in the nation's history, a higher number of non-White first-time students are enrolled in kindergarten compared with White students. The shift comes as the nation's public schools have enrolled surging numbers of Latino and Asian American children in recent years. According to the National Center for Education Statistics (2014), Latino children in particular will account for 25.8% of American public K–12 students this school year and 28.5% in the 2021–2022 academic year. In the 2009–2010 academic year, 22.8% of U.S. students were Latino, according to the National Center for Education Statistics. Moreover, Whites are projected to make up 49.8% of public school students in the United States this year and 46.9% in the 2021–2022 academic year but will then experience steady declines in subsequent years (National Center for Education Statistics, 2014). In short, the continued failure on the nation's part to effectively educate its fastest-growing, and soon to be largest, segments of the population has serious implications for the long-term political, economic, and social prosperity of the country.

SALIENCE OF POSTSECONDARY EDUCATION IN THE 21ST CENTURY

The previously mentioned state of affairs for the nation's urban youth provides an important context for a discussion about the significance of a college education in the 21st century. According to the U.S. Bureau of Labor Statistics (2015a), persons age 25 and older who have a bachelor's degree had median weekly earnings of $1,101, while those with only a high school diploma had median weekly earnings of $668 in 2014. With the unemployment rate for persons age 25 and older who have a bachelor's degree at 3.5% in 2014, and the unemployment rate for individuals with only a high school diploma at 6%, it becomes easy to see why college degree attainment is significant for economic and social mobility in the United States today.

Disaggregation of the 2014 unemployment rates by educational attainment reveals that the unemployment rate for Whites with only a high school diploma (5.1%) and a bachelor's degree or higher (2.9%) varied significantly from the unemployment rate for Blacks with only a high school diploma (10.7%) and a bachelor's degree or higher (5.2%) and Latinos with only a high school diploma (6.2%) and a bachelor's degree or higher (3.9%)

(U.S. Bureau of Labor Statistics, 2015b). According to a 2011 report from the Georgetown University Center on Education and the Workforce, a worker with only a high school diploma earns $1.3 million over a lifetime while a worker with at least a bachelor's degree earns $2.3 million (Carnevale, Rose, & Cheah, 2011). The glaring gap that exists in rates of employment and earning potential for individuals who have a college degree as opposed to those with only a high school diploma has serious consequences for the U.S. population in the 21st century, but the costs are particularly high for urban communities, where educational attainment is much lower. Thus, the educational disparities facing students of color have not only academic implications but also clear-cut economic effects that have obvious consequences for quality of life.

While the economic impact of college degree attainment is enough cause for concern, troubling data on life expectancy and voter participation for individuals based on education level reveal a more disturbing picture. In their report *Education: It Matters More to Health Than Ever Before*, the Center on Society and Health (2014) asserts that compared with those with a college education, Americans with less education (1) die earlier, (2) live with greater illness, (3) generate higher medical care costs, (4) are less productive at work, (5) experience more psychological distress, and (6) have less healthy lifestyles:

> Across racial and ethnic groups, life expectancy improves with increasing years of education. College graduates live longer than adults with only some college education, and in particular, those with even some years of college education and no Bachelor's degree live longer than those with no education beyond high school. (p. 4)

From a health standpoint the connections between health and education have always been clear. Higher educational levels have been equated with a number of positive health outcomes (Pampel, Krueger, & Denney, 2010). A 2013 report from the National Research Council and the Institute of Medicine (2013) cites socioecological factors, along with unhealthy behaviors and deficiencies in the health care system, as leading explanations for the "health disadvantage" of the United States. Moreover, the report cites education as one of the primary ecological factors that must be improved if overall health quality in the United States is to be enhanced. Zimmerman and Woolf (2014) reinforce the health-education connection in a recent report sponsored by the Institute of Medicine:

> Increasing attention is focused on the need to address social inequity in order to address health inequities, understanding the links between broad upstream factors such as education and health outcomes becomes a critical challenge.

Awareness of the importance of education might help drive investment in education and improvements in educational (and health) policy. (p. 2)

In the political arena, there are also salient connections between education and political participation. Approximately 38% of individuals with a high school diploma equivalent or less reported voting in the 2012 presidential election, in contrast with 75% of individuals with a bachelor's degree. And while some may attribute voter participation levels by education to a host of factors in any given election year, the fact remains that higher voter participation rates have consistently been strongly correlated with education levels (Levin, 2005). Jane Junn of the Eagleton Institute of Politics at Rutgers University notes, "Education is the cornerstone of democracy because it aids in the cognitive, ideological and strategic development of democratic citizens, allowing voters to acquire political information, deliberate about the issues, voice perspectives and engage in politics" (Levin, 2005, pp. 18–19). Thus, not only are the economic benefits of education clear, but the political participation implications are too important to ignore as well.

The economic, health, and civic implications for a postsecondary education in the 21st century are clear. Given the marginalized status of urban communities in the United States and the consequences of an inadequate education, it is imperative that educational researchers, leaders, and practitioners think long and hard about the educational success of historically marginalized populations. Fortunately, a considerable amount of initiatives and scholarship has focused almost entirely on finding and enacting strategies for academic success for urban youth. Yet there remains a great deal more to understand when it comes to the link between pre-K–12 schools and postsecondary institutions and the role they play in supporting academic excellence among low-income youth of color from urban communities.

URBAN YOUTH IN POSTSECONDARY INSTITUTIONS OF HIGHER EDUCATION

Clearly, the previously mentioned data speak to the ongoing need to address opportunities for historically marginalized groups and to engage in an analysis of the structural constraints that continue to reproduce inequality in college attainment. To highlight the discrepancies even further, issues that must be explored along racial and ethnic lines are the types of postsecondary institutions that students believe are even at their disposal given their academic profile. According to a report titled *Separate and Unequal: How Higher Education Reinforces the Intergenerational Reproduction of White Racial Privilege* researchers at the Georgetown University Center on Education and the Workforce discovered that although Black and Latino students' enrollment in postsecondary education has increased more rapidly than that of their White counterparts over the past several decades, representation remains a critical issue at the nation's top institutions of higher education (Carnevale & Strohl, 2013). The report found that Whites are significantly overrepresented in the nation's 468 most selective and well-funded colleges and are increasingly absent from the less selective, open-access 2- and 4-year colleges, which admit a majority of their applicants. Conversely, Black and Latino students are highly concentrated at 3,250 of these open-access colleges. Between 1995 and 2009, freshman enrollment of Black and Latino students increased by 73% and 107%, respectively, while freshman enrollment of Whites increased by only 15%. Furthermore, the large majority of new White enrollments—more than 80%—has been at the top 468 colleges, while more than 70% of new African American and Hispanic enrollments have been at open-access colleges. More than 30% of Black and Latino students with a high school grade point average of 3.5 or higher attended community colleges and only 22% of Whites with a similar GPA attended the same level of schooling. Moreover, only 57% of minority students with SAT scores higher than 1200 out of 1600 (the SAT scoring scale changed to a maximum of 2400 points in 2005) eventually received some sort of certificate or degree, compared with 77% of Whites with similar scores.

An example of such racial inequity is found in Texas, where in 2014 approximately 26.6 million Latinos made up approximately 39.2% of the population, African Americans made up 11.5%, and Whites made up 43.5%. Enrollment in higher education was approximately 1.6 million Latinos, or 33.3% of the student population, with African Americans composing 14.3%, and Whites 38.2%, a presumably representative sample of the state's demographics (Texas Higher Education Coordinating Board, 2015). However, a different trend is evident in the state's top colleges and universities. Texas has three universities classified as large, public, highest research activity institutions: the University of Houston; Texas A&M University; and the University of Texas, Austin. At the University of Houston, total undergraduate enrollment of 31,734 in 2014, Latino students comprised 31.3% of the student population, African Americans comprised 11.9% of the student population, and Whites comprised 27.2% of the student population. At Texas A&M University, of the total undergraduate enrollment of 44,647 in 2014, Latino students composed 20.9%, African Americans 3.3%, and Whites 65.4%. And at the University of Texas, Austin, of a total undergraduate enrollment of 39,523 in 2014, Latino students were 22.7% of the student population, African Americans were 4.8%, and Whites were 46.2% (Texas Higher Education Coordinating

Board, 2015). The collective underrepresentation of students of color at the top universities in Texas highlights some of the challenges faced by students of color in higher education. When coupled with data that demonstrate that only 10% of economically disadvantaged 8th-graders in 2003 received a higher education degree or certificate in Texas, a more complete picture is formed about how urban youth fare in institutions of higher education. However, to better understand the true nature of the education pipeline for urban youth, an examination of the obstacles that these students face beyond mere representation becomes increasingly important.

OBSTACLES TO POSTSECONDARY EDUCATION

Despite increased enrollments and completion over the past several decades (U.S. Census Bureau, 1990, 2000, 2010), there has been no significant change in the college achievement gap between Black and White students (Frey, 2013). And the gaps are not explained solely by socioeconomic status. Even when controlled for socioeconomic status, sizable gaps are still persistent in educational attainment across racial lines (Frey, 2013; Howard, 2010). Black and Latino students are less likely to enroll in college than are their more affluent peers who tend to come from more educated households (typically White). Those who do enroll tend to be concentrated in 2-year or less selective and less resourced 4-year colleges with significantly lower success rates (Moore & Shulock, 2010; Perna et al., 2008). Society and the education system play a huge role in the perpetuation of these inequalities through a culture that "advantages students who are generally already advantaged" (Milner, 2013; Park & Eagan, 2011, p. 2369). Disadvantaged Black students in particular who do reach the college campus struggle with how to make up for the "educational deficits resulting from years of systemic discrimination and blocked educational opportunities, while meeting the daily challenges of rigorous academic programs that make no allowances for the cumulative, debilitating effects of historic and continuing racial discrimination" (Allen & Solorzano, 2001, p. 240). As a result, Black and Latino students are the most likely to enter and not complete college (Frey, 2013). In this cycle of inequality, students "who have been excluded from educational opportunities over the past centuries . . . continue to be at or near the bottom of the achievement gap" (Howard, 2010, p. 11).

The good news is that the desire to attain a college degree has become almost universal among high school students. More and more students see a college degree as essential to improving their earning potential in an increasingly competitive global economy. While this may seem insignificant, a considerable degree of the discourse that surrounds urban youth and postsecondary education has been dominated by deficit frameworks that assert that students of color are less interested in academics and have low aspirations both academically and professionally. As the authors of *Barriers to College Attainment: Lessons from Chicago* note, "The primary issue in college access is no longer building college aspirations, but building a clear path for students to achieve their goals" (Nagaoka, Roderick, & Coca, 2009, p. 1). Factors that relate to understanding the barriers to postsecondary education for urban youth of color have received considerable attention in education research for several decades (Coleman et al., 1966; Fordham & Ogbu, 1986; Gándara, 1995; Gay & Abrahams, 1974; Orfield, Losen, Wald, & Swanson, 2002). Scholars have highlighted several major challenges that impede urban students' access to higher education—poor academic preparation, students' difficulties navigating the college enrollment process, and the declining real value of financial aid combined with rising college costs.

Academic Preparation/Unequal Curriculum

A major factor contributing to the previously mentioned distribution of students at U.S. colleges and universities has to do with eligibility and competitiveness that are directly influenced by students' academic preparation. Urban youth of color are more likely to attend majority student-of-color K–12 schools where there are higher levels of concentrated poverty than their White peers (Orfield, 1996). Further, majority-White pre-K–12 schools in the United States are overwhelmingly middle class and are more likely to have high-quality veteran teachers, rigorous academic curricula, and social capital that translates into increased chances to take advantage of extracurricular and out-of-school learning opportunities (Darling Hammond, 2010). This intense segregation of low-income students of color in urban schools becomes a critical factor when trying to understand the troubling postsecondary outlook for marginalized urban communities.

Data from the National Center for Education Statistics (2013b) continue to show that Black and Latino students attend college at significantly lower rates than those of their White peers. While it is true that higher numbers of African American and Latino students from urban communities have been graduating from high school over the past several decades and that an increasing number of these students is enrolling in institutions of higher education, far too many of these students do not find their way into more selective 4-year colleges and universities. For example, 58% of all New York City 9th-graders graduated after 4 years of high school in 2006. Only 44% of 2006 New York City high school graduates enrolled directly into a 4-year college or university, while 15% enrolled in a 2-year institution of higher education in 2010 (Research Alliance for New York City Schools, 2014). Approximately 28% of 2006 New York City high school graduates enrolled in a City University of New York (CUNY) college directly after high school, effectively making the CUNY system a destination for almost half of all New York City high school graduates. Important to note here is that this cohort of CUNY enrollees was not evenly distributed across CUNY tiers: Of the total, 13% enrolled in CUNY community colleges, 5% in second-tier institutions, and 11% in top-tier institutions (Research Alliance for New York City Schools, 2014). Trend data demonstrate that cohorts at top-tier CUNY institutions have become increasingly White and Asian over the past decade, while Black and Latino students are increasingly overrepresented in the system's second-tier and community college institutions (Treschan & Mehrotra, 2012). This is undoubtedly an effect of the gap that exists in the type of diploma (i.e., academic preparation) that students leave New York City high schools with upon graduation. In 2009, 61% of all New York City 12th-graders graduated after 4 years of high school. Only 17% of these students completed high school with a Regents diploma with advanced designation, while 41% completed high school with just a Regents diploma and 3% with a local diploma. This means that two-thirds of New York City graduates did not complete the more rigorous and comprehensive coursework (i.e., taking additional coursework in a language other than English or career and technical education or the arts and passing two additional Regents exams in math and one additional Regents exam in science) required for the advanced designation diploma in 2009.

As highlighted earlier, educational researchers have spent a notable amount of time investigating some of the factors that affect the lack of preparation urban students of color receive during their pre-K–12 education. Compelling evidence highlights how students of color are disproportionately "tracked" into general and special education courses and are less likely to be placed in the honors and Advanced Placement courses that would make them competitively eligible for more selective colleges and universities (Oakes, 2005). Lisa Delpit (2006, 2008, 2013) and others argue that this underrepresentation is fueled, in part, by the lowered expectations that a majority White, monolingual, and middle-class teaching force has of urban students of color. In her book *"Multiplication Is for White People,"* Delpit (2013) highlights several examples of how students of color from urban communities receive less demanding class assignments and homework even when taking the same-level class and when working from the same textbook as their White and more affluent peers. The examples provided by Delpit only reinforce the seminal work of Anyon (1980), who, decades ago, noted that the more diverse and working class a school is, the more likely its students are to receive an education that de-emphasizes critical thinking and instead focuses on rote memorization with few opportunities to engage in knowledge creation processes that prepare them for the demands of a college curriculum.

Navigating the College Application and Enrollment Process

A substantial body of research suggests that low-income students of color often do not have the same type of access to information and guidance needed to effectively navigate the college application process as their more affluent and White peers (Cabrera & La Nasa, 2000a, 2000b; Gonzalez, Stoner, & Jovel, 2003; Howard, 2003; McDonough, 1997; Person & Rosenbaum, 2006; Schneider & Stevenson, 1999; Stanton-Salazar, 2001; Wimberly, 2002). In "Potholes on the Road to College," Roderick, Coca, and Nagaoka (2011) argue that there are two mechanisms by which "differential access to guidance, information, and norms for four-year college attendance may contribute to observed differences by race/ethnicity and income in college enrollment among similarly qualified students" (p. 180). The first mechanism is whether seniors effectively take the steps to apply to and enroll in a 4-year college. Roderick and colleagues (2011) point to the work of Avery and Kane (2004), who studied seniors at Boston public schools and in nearby suburban schools to highlight that among students who planned to attend a 4-year college, 91% of the suburban sample obtained an application from the college they were interested in attending by the fall of their senior year compared with only a little more than half the Boston public school sample. Only 18% of the Boston sample versus 41% of the suburban sample had even applied to a 4-year college by the fall. The second mechanism that Roderick and colleagues (2011) point to is whether students conduct a broad college search and do not constrain their college choice. Low-income urban students of color often rely too heavily on their own familial and friendship networks to have sufficient information about processes relating to college applications and enrollment (Hearn, 1991; Kim & Schneider, 2005; Person & Rosenbaum, 2006), and "limited information results in many urban students focusing their entire college search within traditional feeder patterns, largely public, two-year, or nonselective and somewhat selective colleges" (Roderick et al., 2011, p. 180). Urban students of color often lack access to college counselors and the social capital that could enable them to successfully navigate the college application and enrollment process.

Federally funded TRiO programs and other institution- and community-based initiatives have attempted to address some of the persistent challenges faced by low-income, first-generation students who come from urban communities during the college application and enrollment process with the hope of making colleges and universities more accessible. The important role that programs like TRiO have played in creating more pathways to higher education for urban students will be discussed in a later chapter; however, it is also important to highlight some of the steps being taken by colleges and universities in addition to state lawmakers to increase the number of low-income students of color who enroll in college. In fall 2007, leaders from public higher education systems across the country launched the Access-to-Success Initiative (A2S). This initiative represents one of a few concerted efforts by public higher education systems to address the underenrollment and persistence rates of underrepresented low-income students of color. The 22 A2S systems represent 312 2-year and 4-year campuses and serve more than 3.5 million students (Education Trust, 2012). Together, these systems educate about 20% of students attending public institutions nationally, including nearly 40% of underrepresented low-income students of color attending public 4-year institutions across the country. Because of the large number of higher education systems and varying demographic contexts, initiatives and institutional practices look different across A2S systems. Nevertheless, increasing numbers of Black and Latino students are enrolling in A2S systems (Education Trust, 2012).

Through legislative efforts to address structural and institutional barriers facing urban students, urban students of color presumably have better access to the nation's institutions of higher education. For example, in 1997 Texas House Bill 588, known as the "Texas Top 10% Rule," guaranteed that students who graduated in the top 10% of their high school class received automatic admission to any state-funded university regardless of the student's standardized test scores. This rule is similar to California's Eligibility in the Local Context (ELC) policy, which was implemented for fall 2001 admission to the University of California (UC) system. This new path made the top 4% of students in each California high school eligible for UC if they completed specified academic coursework by the end of their junior year. To be considered for admission and to enroll at UC, ELC students have to apply for admission and complete UC-required courses and the standardized testing requirement by the end of their senior year, which, in turn, guarantees applicants admission to UC, though not necessarily in the program or at the campus of their choice. At the heart of policies like Texas Top 10% and California's ELC is the idea that creating pathways to higher education that are based on students' schooling context increases opportunities for urban students of color to matriculate into 4-year colleges and universities. However, urban students of color remain woefully underrepresented in the University of Texas system as well as at UC, especially at these systems' top-tier, flagship universities. Roderick and colleagues (2011) point to the shortcomings of these policies; evaluators of the Texas Top 10% law found that although the policy led students from a larger number of high schools to apply to the Texas flagship universities, the increase in applications was largely driven by applicants from more affluent high schools and not low-income urban schools (Koffman & Tienda, 2008; Long, Saenz, & Tienda, 2010). They conclude that the admissions guarantee did little to raise flagship applications from poor high schools. As well intentioned as some of these policies are, urban students of color still face manifold barriers when it comes to applying and enrolling in colleges and universities.

Funding the Cost of Higher Education

Another significant barrier for urban students of color is the increasing cost of higher education. The average cost of undergraduate tuition, room, and board for full-time students at degree-granting institutions of higher education in the United States during the 1982–1983 academic year was $3,877. Thirteen years later, the cost had swelled to $20,234 (Kena et al., 2015). The increasing cost of a higher education degree has contributed to a troubling trend in the relationship between family income and eventual degree attainment. In 2013, the Education Trust found that while roughly 8 in 10 young people in families with an annual income of $99,000 or more earn a bachelor's degree by age 24, only 1 in 9 young people from families earning less than $33,000 a year do so. The trust notes:

> During the 1940s and early '50s, increases in the price of college were manageable because median family income grew even faster. But that dynamic stabilized through the '60s and '70s, reversed around 1980, and came to a crashing halt in the beginning of this century. Today, not only is tuition rising faster than for generations past, it is and it feels less affordable as a function of a decline in family wealth. (p. 4)

Highlighting factors such as significant state divestment from higher education, a relatively stagnant supply of postsecondary institutions, and increased, yet underinformed, consumer demand, the Education Trust points to inefficient funding processes, inadequate need-based aid, and high student loan debt as the main culprits that disadvantage low-income urban students of color when it comes to funding their higher education. It is worth noting that several institutions, among them Harvard, Stanford, and Duke, have developed tuition assistance programs that cover the full cost of college for students from low-income families without the expectation that students or their families take out loans. However, an analysis of

Harvard's tuition assistance program reveals that the real impact of such policies account for a very small increase (if any) in the number of low-income students who join the freshman class of these institutions of higher education (Vedantam, 2013).

California Context

In 1960, California adopted its Master Plan for Higher Education, which organized the state's higher education structure. The broad intent of the plan was to configure an interconnected set of institutions that would provide access to higher education for all Californians (California State Department of Education, 1960). However, political policies resulted in dramatic declines in the university admission and enrollment rates of underrepresented students, particularly Black and Latino students from urban communities. In 1978, *Regents of the University of California v. Bakke* and, in 1979, *United Steelworkers v. Weber* became the first U.S. Supreme Court cases to weaken previously enacted policies and programs focusing on equity via affirmative action (Lindsay & Justiz, 2001). While the *Bakke* decision maintained that race preferences in which spaces are set aside for students or potential employees of a preferred category are unconstitutional, race could lawfully be considered a criterion for academic admissions (Jones, 1996). The 1990s witnessed numerous challenges to affirmative action programs and policies, including *Podberesky v. Kirwin* and *Adarand Constructors Inc. v. Pena*. In 1996, California's Proposition 209 was approved. Originally, the Board of Regents of the University of California passed Board of Regents Order SP-1 (1994), which prohibited the university from using affirmative action in student admissions, financial aid, and the awarding of contracts. Not long after the passage of Order SP-1UC, Ward Connerly, a regent at UC, led an effort to add Proposition 209 as an amendment to the state constitution, to prohibit public institutions from considering race, sex, color, ethnicity, or national origin in public employment, education, and contracting. Following the ban on race-based admissions by the regents and the passage of Proposition 209, the number of underrepresented students enrolled at UC plummeted—"the abrupt drop in Black and Latino enrollments in California raised the specter of a return to 'whites only' times, not just on college campuses but also in the professions and in the next generation of state leadership" (Lindsay & Justiz, 2001, p. 56). The decline in African American and Latino admissions was drastic in the UC system, particularly at the Los Angeles and Berkeley campuses. Between 1994 and 2014, admission rates for Black applicants declined by 41 points at UC Berkeley, compared with 25 points for all applicants combined; 46 points at UCLA, compared with 34 points for all applicants combined; and 44 points at UC San Diego, compared with 35 points for all applicants combined (University of California Office of the President, 2014). In 2014, at least two-thirds of Black applicants were denied admission to six of UC's nine undergraduate campuses: Berkeley, Los Angeles, San Diego, Davis, Irvine, and Santa Barbara. By comparison, at least two-thirds of White applicants were denied admission to only three campuses.

The dramatic decline in Black and Latino enrollment has impelled higher education administrators to vigorously pursue alternate ways to maintain diversity within the newly created legal and political boundaries. This context served as a primer for the creation of the VIP Scholars program as a way to remedy this issue. The Campaign for College Opportunity (2015) reports that many urban students of color face significant barriers, through no fault of their own, on their pathway to a college degree, including:

- Low income
- Attended a low-performing high school
- First in their families to attend college
- Placement into pre-college-level courses
- Insufficient state funding for colleges/universities
- Insufficient college advising and support
- Insufficient financial aid

It is these barriers and challenges that the VIP Scholars and other high-school-to-college programs seek to disrupt. The importance of identifying obstacles in the high-school-to-college process is to seek ways to offset the gaping holes in the educational pipeline.

CONCLUSION

Throughout this book, the authors address the importance of academic support, mentorship, and parent/community/university engagement, in addition to the significance of culturally and socially relevant curriculum in guiding urban youth onto viable postsecondary pathways. While this book places one high-school-to-college program at the center of analysis, broader discussions about college access, social justice, and equity are taken up in an effort to contribute to an ongoing dialogue about what schools, parents, and universities can do to best meet the needs of students from urban schools. Many programs and models exist to meet the needs of students from urban schools who rightfully deserve opportunities to gain access to higher education. However, we feel strongly that the model and framing of the issue of college access offered in this book can play an important role in advancing scholarship and programming related to the educational pipeline of students from urban communities.

Two

Response to the College Access Problem

VIP Scholars—a Social Justice Approach

Jonli D. Tunstall, Ashley V. Williams,
Justyn K. Patterson, and Jerry Morrison

College access programs provide students from underserved communities and underrepresented backgrounds with the information and tools necessary to attain higher education. In 2005, the VIP Scholars (VIPS) program was created in response to the declining number of students from urban or underrepresented communities at selective institutions following the passage of Proposition 209 in California. One of the primary aspects that will set the VIPS program apart from others is its mission to further develop student participants' critical consciousness, resulting in students' active engagement in addressing educational inequalities in urban schools and communities. This chapter will first provide an overview of effective college access programs that work with students of color. We will then provide an overview of the VIPS program and the theoretical framework that informs how the program has operated for the past 10 years as a social justice college access program. Last, we will outline the explicit ways in which the social justice framework VIPS uses remains a key component that makes it unique from many other college access programs focused on underserved student populations.

COLLEGE ACCESS PROGRAMS

Today, approximately 50 years after the creation of the first educational outreach programs—or college access programs—an estimated 1,650 such programs exist in the United States (Domina, 2009; Swail, 2000). These programs were intended to lessen the educational disenfranchisement of underserved students by increasing college readiness and exposing underrepresented students to postsecondary educational opportunities (Pitre & Pitre, 2009; Tierney & Jun, 2001). Evolving from federal initiatives, nearly 60% of all outreach programs are sponsored by colleges and universities, 16% by the K–12 system, 13% by community-based organizations and nonprofits, and 14% by other entities, with funding from federal and state government, private business, foundations, and other sources (Swail, 2000). For nearly half the programs, the primary site of services is a college campus, another 35% take place on a K–12 campus, and the remainder occur at community centers and other locales (Swail, 2000). Over 90% of programs target students in middle school and beyond, with more than 50% of all programs targeting high school students (Swail, 2000). The federal government commits over $1 billion to federal outreach programs (Swail & Perna, 2002), with states like California consistently committing tens of millions of dollars to outreach efforts (Swail & Perna, 2002; Torres, 2004) every year, in large part because of the persistent challenges that some students face in K–12 education. Underrepresented students struggle against numerous impediments to their pursuit of postsecondary education, including: minimal critical social and economic capital, inequality of resources, lack of access to rigorous academic curriculum, scarcity of qualified teachers, inadequate academic and social support, tracking, lack of peer support, poor counseling, and lack of a college-going culture (Burris, Wiley, Welner, & Murphy, 2008; Farmer-Hinton & Adams, 2006; McKown & Weinstein, 2008; Oakes & Lipton, 2003). College access programs often provide college preparatory services to underrepresented students in schools that do not have the capacity or expertise to do so.

What Do College Access Programs Do?

Generally, college access programs adopt one of two models. Most programs are student-centered and provide services to participants with a targeted-cohort approach in which a subset of the school population is identified because they are low-income, first-generation college-going, from an underrepresented minority, or low achieving academically (Domina, 2009; Perna, 2002). Student-centered programs operate with the underlying assumption that students make a rational choice about whether to pursue postsecondary education based upon the likelihood that they will be admitted and experience success in college, as well as the returns they will receive because of their educational attainment (Domina, 2009). Student-centered programs offer an array of services that may include some combination of academic support (e.g., tutoring), college counseling, and parent support. These programs are designed to increase the likelihood of student academic success and affect the academic expectations of students and their parents (Glennie, Dalton, & Knapp, 2014; Myers, Olsen, Seftor, Young, & Tuttle, 2004; Perna, 2002; Swail, 2000). The underlying assumption is that if students experience educational success, have accurate college information, and develop a connection to the college atmosphere, they will be more likely to pursue education beyond high school.

An alternate approach to the student-centered program is a schoolwide approach to college access programming. This approach holds the philosophy that educational aspiration and achievement is a function of the students' environment and social influences (Domina, 2009). The resulting programs are developed and implemented with the assumption that academic performance and college aspirations result from teacher expectations and peer influence, which differs from the "rational choice" framework adopted by student-centered programs. School-centered programs attempt to affect the entire school community by creating an overall academic environment that promotes student success (Domina, 2009). They disseminate college information to all students at a particular school or in a specified grade level, working with school administrators and counselors to improve their familiarity with college information, and advocating that advanced courses be made more available to all students. The success of these programs depends upon changes along multiple domains operating in a school, including teacher expectations and beliefs, effective professional development and support for instructors, efficacy of administrative leadership, and funding, to name just a few. School-centered programs are less prevalent than student-centered programs because the former are dependent on the synergy created from these various domains and therefore their impacts may take several years to realize (Gándara, 2002).

Both student-centered and school-centered approaches recognize that college information and counseling are vital to student academic achievement and educational aspiration. Scholars have long identified lack of adequate counseling as a hindrance for underrepresented students in their pursuit of higher education (Oakes & Guiton, 1995; Oakes & Lipton, 2003). Underrepresented students in particular tend to not see their counselors as allies or supporters, but instead as impediments who prevent access to college preparatory courses and information (Gándara, 2002; McDonough, 1997). The lack of sound counseling results in students being tracked into lower-level courses, thereby limiting their exposure to a college preparatory curriculum, causing poorer performance on required standardized tests, and leading to lower rates of college enrollment (Gándara, 2002). By including a college counseling component, access programs are attempting to raise college awareness and increase students' predisposition to attend college.

Research also reveals that parental involvement is a key component in a student's likelihood to enroll in college (Fan & Chen, 2001; Herndon & Hirt, 2004; Hossler & Stage, 1992). Many underserved communities, however, lack the cultural capital—knowledge of how the educational system works—and social capital, that is, access to important social networks, that White students can obtain (Bourdieu, 1977; Farmer-Hinton & Adams, 2006). More affluent parents typically have a better understanding of how to use a school's resources to the advantage of their children, while low-income parents often do not possess the same social capital, and therefore the same access to resources and support, as their more affluent counterparts (Lin, 2000; Stanton-Salazar & Dornbusch, 1995). Some college access programs attempt to address these inequalities by creating a parent component for their programs. Many parents of program participants have limited to no college experience, and access programs provide opportunities for parents to learn about college and understand that college can be an option for their children (Fan & Chen, 2001; Tierney & Auerbach, 2005). Programs also provide parents with information about educational opportunities and teach parents how to monitor their children's educational progress. Perna (2002) found that 75% of the programs included in her study of 1,100 programs included a parent component, with approximately 25% of them being mandatory.

Hossler and Gallagher's (1987) study, as cited by Perna (2002), provides a commonly accepted three-stage framework for understanding college enrollment and the manner in which access programs structure their program offerings. In Stage 1, *predisposition*, students decide whether or not they want to attend college as opposed to pursuing other options such as entering the workforce or joining the military. A student's predisposition toward college enrollment and graduation is related to the social and cultural capital that he or she can obtain (Bourdieu, 1977; McDonough, 1997). Lower-income students and students of color are generally at a distinct disadvantage when seeking access to higher education because their environments often do not grant them access to the same resources and connections that their more privileged or White peers may have. In their study, Gándara and Bial (2001) found that 28 of 33 programs that they surveyed included a college counseling component, which can be linked directly to students' expectation, or predisposition, when it comes to attending college and earning a degree (Gándara, 2002; Oakes, 2003; Perna, 2006). College counseling plays an instrumental role in increasing access to higher education and raising students' academic expectations (McDonough, 2005a; Oakes, 2003).

In Stage 2, *search*, students seek out college information and decide where to apply. The search stage of the college choice process entails both the processing and gathering of information about college and specific institutions

(Perna, 2002). Access programs use various methods to facilitate this process, including campus tours and visits, meetings with college professors and students, and college fairs (Cabrera & La Nasa, 2001; Kirst & Venezia, 2004; Swail, 2000). Approximately 46% of programs offer their services on a college campus, thereby creating a connection between program participants and the university setting, and in more than 40% of programs students are guided through the arduous process of identifying colleges and completing and submitting applications (Gándara & Bial, 2001; Perna, 2002).

In Stage 3, *choice*, students select the institution to attend. College choice decisions are based on numerous factors, not the least of which is academic eligibility. Many programs offer students academic enrichment opportunities before or after school, on the weekends, and during the summer to make up for the deficiencies they experience within the school system (Gándara, 2002; Myers et al., 2004). Among these enrichment opportunities are workshops covering topics ranging from critical thinking skills, to study skills training, to mathematics and science instruction, to reading and writing instruction (Swail & Perna, 2002).

UPWARD BOUND AND GEAR UP

Some educational outreach programs of note that are addressing the issue of college access and success around the nation are Upward Bound and GEAR UP. Upward Bound targets first-generation college-going and low-income students as potential participants in their program (Myers et al., 2004). In the last full report of Upward Bound in 2006, there were 761 Upward Bound projects nationwide servicing more than 56,000 students (Seftor, Mamun, & Schirm, 2009). In 2006, Upward Bound received federal funding of $267 million, or $4,800 per student (Seftor et al., 2009). Myers's (2004) longitudinal study of Upward Bound evaluated 67 programs nationwide and shows that program activities address the predisposition, search, and choice phases of the college enrollment framework. In Upward Bound's effort to foster a predisposition for college, students attended an average of 66 counseling sessions and 50 college preparation workshops during their time in the program. Upward Bound addresses Stage 2, search, by conducting college tours and fieldtrips. On average, students attend 13 fieldtrips throughout their time in the program. Upward Bound programs are university based and the majority of services take place on college campuses, also fostering a connection to higher education and facilitating the critical college information-gathering process. While Upward Bound provides support in the first two stages of the college enrollment process, the bulk of their work is geared toward improving students' academic achievement and opening the door to more choice in applying to colleges (Stage 3). On average, students participated in 265 academic sessions in English, foreign languages, math, computers, science, electives, and other subjects.

Another program of note is the U.S. Department of Education's Gaining Early Awareness and Readiness for Undergraduate Programs (GEAR UP). GEAR UP is an early intervention college access program created to assist nearly one million low-income middle school students and their families in preparing for college (Cabrera et al., 2006). Unlike student-centered, small-cohort model programs like Upward Bound, GEAR UP takes a school-centered outreach approach and services an entire grade level at project schools. Since it began in 1999, GEAR UP has received over $1.8 billion of federal support (Ward, 2006). A key component of the GEAR UP model is the required partnership between high-poverty middle schools, colleges, and universities, and community and business entities (Cabrera et al., 2006). Data from a national study of GEAR UP show that the program serves a racially diverse group of students (30% Black, 36% Latino, 26% White, 3% Asian, and 5% Native American). The schools that participate generally serve a higher low-income population than the national average. A requirement for participation is that 50% or more of the school's student population is eligible for the National School Lunch Program (NSLP), with GEAR UP partnerships reporting that approximately 65% of their students are NSLP eligible.

GEAR UP activities vary significantly between projects but fall into several broad categories. The most common service was *academic support*. Approximately 43% of student participants reported receiving homework help while in the program. While homework assistance was the most prevalent type of academic support, 28% of students received math tutoring, 19% received English tutoring, and 15% received tutoring in science. Academic assistance most often took place in small groups during the school day, although some projects structured after-school programs, Saturday academies, and summer programs for their students.

In order to support the predisposition and search phases of the college access pathway, GEAR UP invests heavily in the *college counseling and information* component of their program. Nearly half the participants reported receiving one-on-one counseling on preparing for high school, and 34% reported receiving counseling about planning for college; almost 60% of participants visited a college campus. Most projects also hosted college fairs on their campuses for their entire student body. These events included poster presentations from various universities and workshops hosted by university staff and students.

While GEAR UP invests heavily in providing students with college counseling and information, providing parents with information is a central program component. A *parent information* component makes up the third most common component of GEAR UP projects nationwide. More than half the programs provide parents with general college information, while others developed more comprehensive college counseling programs for their parents.

While college access programs like Upward Bound and GEAR UP focus on providing high school students with pertinent college information, they fall short of providing a transformative experience that can have a positive effect on not only the student but also the community as a whole. By contrast, the VIP Scholars program inclusion of a social justice educational theoretical framework has driven the work of the program since its inception.

VIP SCHOLARS PROGRAM

The Vice Provost Initiative for Pre-College Scholars (VIPS) program was established in 2005 in response to the declining number of underrepresented students, specifically Black students, admitted and enrolled at competitive 4-year universities. In collaboration with key stakeholders at a large public research institution in Los Angeles, this university-based program was designed to help prepare historically underrepresented students to become competitively eligible for baccalaureate work at selective universities and to encourage pursuit of graduate and professional education. VIPS aims to increase the number of underserved students from Los Angeles County who are competitively eligible for admission to prestigious universities through an array of academic programs composed of college counseling, mentoring, student leadership, academic advising, and summer residential programs. The program espouses both a student-centered cohort approach and schoolwide approach working with the general population of students at 10 partnering high schools. The schoolwide approach consists of a partnership between the university and the Los Angeles and Pasadena Unified School Districts, with 10 selected urban schools that have high populations of underrepresented students from low-income families. The 10 partner schools were selected based not only on student demographics within the school but also on relationships that program leadership had with the school districts that allowed for access into the school sites.

VIP Scholars uses a multifaceted approach that engages not only the high school students but also their families, high school staff, and current university students who function as mentors. VIPS program activities, among them Mentoring, Buddy Days, Saturday Academies, Parent Night, Campus Clubs, and annual summer programs, address the predisposition, search, and choice phases of the college enrollment framework (Hossler & Gallagher, 1987; Perna, 2002). During the academic year, two complementary programs are organized. The schoolwide approach is focused on working with a large group of students in each of the 10 partner high schools, and the other with a smaller group of cohort students who engage in summer programming and quarterly Saturday Academies at the university.

Mentoring is an important cornerstone of the VIPS program and undergraduate mentors conduct a majority of the work at partnering school sites. Weekly, VIPS mentors visit their assigned partner school, where they meet with general-population students and VIPS cohort students. The program's mentors are predominately low-income, first-generation, underrepresented undergraduates (and graduate students) with diverse educational backgrounds. Many mentors are former VIPS participants who have returned to their alma mater and are thus able to more easily navigate their school site. Mentors works closely with high school counselors to share college information, provide professional development, conduct workshops, and encourage a college-going culture. Mentors review students' grades, track progress for taking standardized tests, and guide students through the college application process. In addition, mentors support students in advocating for grades and courses with counselors and teachers while also discussing various policy changes within their respective high schools. This type of advocacy serves as an integral piece to effective relationships between youth and adults to promote positive development (Ginwright & James, 2002; Jarrett, Sullivan, & Watkins, 2005; Larson, Walker, & Pearce, 2005). Undergraduate mentors are also trained to conduct one-on-one check-ins with youth, to not only assess their academic progress but also understand the impact that students' lived experience outside the classroom—family and community influences and experiences—has on their educational experience. In the VIPS general-program schoolwide approach, mentors serve an average of 150 students at each participating high school for a total of 1,150 students each year.

In order to continue providing students with college counseling and information, VIPS full-time staff and trained undergraduate mentors work with partner high school faculty and staff to host events, such as Parent Nights and Buddy Days. At Parent Nights, university students and staff host an evening event at the various school sites specifically for family members in order to share college information. The university and high school partners offer families food and child care during the event to make it easier for families to attend. Buddy Days are unique opportunities for high school students to become college students for a day. Each high school student is paired with a university undergraduate student based on academic and career interests with a goal of giving students a real college-life experience. High school students shadow a college student for the day and tour the campus, attend lectures, visit the residential halls, and meet with university students and staff to discuss the college experience of undergraduate students. The program also collaborates with other programs such as Students Heightening Academic Performance through Education (SHAPE) and student organizations on the university's campus including Senior Saturdays, a 2-day workshop designed to assist high school seniors in Los Angeles County with their college applications.

In addition to focusing on college guidance and outreach activities, mentors work to recruit and select high school students who will be included in the next cohort of VIP Scholars. Counselors and teachers at each high school nominate eligible students who could benefit in some way from participation the program. Over 175 students subsequently apply each year from partner schools and 50 students along with their parents/guardians are selected for interviews. Thirty scholars are then selected from across the 10 urban high schools that participate in two academically rigorous residential summer programs that take place at the university, one before students enter 11th grade and the other before the 12th. The Junior Scholars participate in a 2-week summer residential program intended to introduce students to college-level work while also equipping them with writing, study, and time management skills that will assist them in their junior year. If the students remain academically eligible and involved in the program in their junior year, they are invited back to participate in the 5-week summer residential program. In this program, Senior Scholars take two college courses and begin working on the college application process. Since its inception, VIP Scholars summer programs have served 300 high school students. The students selected for the program represent students from low-income and working-class backgrounds and include a variety of students who have different levels of academic achievement, leadership involvement, and family backgrounds.

Throughout the academic year, VIP Scholars and their parents participate in eight mandatory Saturday Academies held on the university campus. Each Saturday Academy focuses on central themes and issues surrounding access to higher education. Students and their parents receive assistance in preparing for college and are trained in skills to help them become better advocates for their education; for many, it is the first substantive college counseling they have received.

As is common with other college access programs, VIPS provides college counseling and information to underserved students, engages parents/families in programming, and includes the college enrollment framework of predisposition, search, and choice (Hossler & Gallagher, 1987; Perna, 2002) in its program structure to address the issue of college access and success. However, VIPS has an intentional focus on social justice and developing critical consciousness in its participants that is woven into every aspect of the program. Through mentoring, classes, workshops, fieldtrips, and other leadership development activities, VIPS seeks to equip student participants for success in college, graduate, and professional school and to make a positive impact on their communities.

VIPS HISTORY AND BACKGROUND

VIP Scholars functions as a social justice college access program. It was established in 2005 in response to the declining number of students of color, specifically African American students, at the university. Aware of the detrimental impact of Proposition 209 on the enrollment of Black students at public universities, two high-ranking university administrators decided that something needed to be done. They knew that it was not that Black students were not smart enough; rather, these students lacked access and opportunity. The administrators recognized that the university needed to do more, but they were not sure what more looked like. They charged a K–12 educator who had had years in the public and private sector with the task of coming up with a solution. The administrators did not have the information, expertise, or time required, and finding someone with the right background in public schools was imperative. To begin laying the foundation for this important work, the founding director of the program brought together key stakeholders on campus—university students, faculty, and staff—who were concerned with and invested in addressing the decline in African American enrollment, not only at their home university but also at colleges and universities across the United States. These key individuals brought with them varying experiences working in K–12 schools as teachers and administrators, faculty, and educational researchers who were involved in extensive research on education issues surrounding African American students. This group also included undergraduate and graduate students and staff who engaged in considerable work with youth and spearheaded numerous education programs for underrepresented students in the K–16 system. These individuals, who brought with them varying experiences, related anecdotes that collectively revealed ways in which African American students were being underserved and inadequately prepared for higher education.

They told of working with students in urban schools who had high hopes of attending UCLA only to discover, once they looked at their transcripts in senior year, that they were missing a foreign language, which made their

4.2 GPA null and void because they had failed to meet the college eligibility requirements. Others told of students who had the grades and SAT scores to attend the university but chose not to apply because they felt the university did not want them or they were not good enough to apply. Other stories were told of students who lived less than 10 miles from the university but had never stepped foot on a college campus. There were other stories of counselors and teachers who had negative ideas about students' ability to reach college and discouraged them from even applying to 4-year colleges. Then there were the students who were tracked their entire lives, in other words, placed into high-ability groups and academic programs as opposed to students who were placed into "vocational" or "general programs" (Oakes, 2005), and therefore carried with them meritocratic notions such as "I'm going to college and those students aren't because they don't try hard enough." Or even once students got to college, they felt inadequate, isolated, and unprepared for the experience of being the only Black student in a classroom of more than 300 students. These experiences were the impetus in creating a program that focused on college access and social justice.

GUIDING PRINCIPLES OF THE VIP SCHOLARS PROGRAM

The establishment of the VIP Scholars program entailed certain key principles grounded in various educational theories that would drive the work of the program. Programs within VIPS are designed to support the experiences of students of color and explore the impact of race, class, and gender on the education system. Distinct from other college access programs is the VIPS program's intentional focus on both college access and social justice. While providing information and experiences to prepare student participants for college and expose them to higher education is important, equally important to the VIPS program is the inclusion of a social justice framework that engages students in a discourse that allows them to learn about their history, culture, and community throughout their participation in the program. This empowers student participants not only to recognize their ability to transform current unjust realities but also to become actively engaged in their schools and communities in meaningful ways.

Critical Pedagogy

Duncan-Andrade and Morrell (2008) argue for the use of pedagogy that investigates and draws from the social contexts of the lives of urban youth. This particular approach to programming draws from students' funds of knowledge, that is, the knowledge and experience students bring with them from their home, their communities, and the popular culture of youth (Gonzalez et al., 2013). The purpose of critical pedagogy is to engage students in the act of what educator-scholar Paolo Freire calls *conscientizacao*, or "learning to perceive social, political and economic contradictions, and to take action against the oppressive elements of reality" (Freire, 1970, p. 17). Critical pedagogy cultivates conscious individuals who are aware of themselves and the social conditions under which they live. It entails not simply offering students new ways to think critically, but is also concerned with providing students with the skills and knowledge necessary for them to take responsibility for intervening in the world they inhabit (Giroux, 2007). Through this engagement, students develop as "transformative intellectuals" (Giroux, 1988) and "cultural workers" (Freire, 1998) who are capable of identifying and addressing the injustices and inequalities of an often oppressive world (Gruenewald, 2003). Through the inclusion of critical pedagogy, students understand history and are empowered by such knowledge and use their insight to overcome various challenges and join with others (Kincheloe, 2007, 2008) to address inequity they see and experience.

Social Justice Youth Development

In his acclaimed *Pedagogy of the Oppressed*, Freire (1970) posits that education can be a process of liberation through *praxis*, the practice of thinking critically about one's world and acting to transform it. The social justice youth development (SJYD) model was developed based on the principle of praxis as integral to the positive development of youth from oppressed communities (Ginwright & Cammarota, 2002). SJYD addresses the institutionalized injustices urban youth experience in economic, political, and social contexts and prepares youth to become agents of change to address these injustices. The ultimate goal of the SJYD model is to create an awareness of social justice for youth in oppressive environments so that they can understand causes of social problems that contribute to oppressive conditions in their lives and those of others in their communities.

SJYD views youth not as problems but as change agents who possess assets and can be assets to the world (Ginwright & Cammarota, 2002; Lerner, Almerigi, Theokas, & Lerner, 2005). SJYD programs are built on five principles: (1) analyzing power in social relationships, (2) making identity central, (3) promoting systemic social change, (4) encouraging collective action, and (5) embracing youth culture (Ginwright & James, 2002). When put into practice, these principles produce outcomes associated with sociopolitical development.

Sociopolitical Development

Through the process of sociopolitical development (SPD), a person becomes increasingly aware of existing social inequities and their history (Watts, Williams, & Jagers, 2003) and gains an understanding of the historical, racial, social, and political factors that influence people's day-to-day challenges and circumstances (Watts, Griffith, & Abdul-Adil, 1998). True SPD occurs when individuals are able to integrate personal experience in different power relationships into a multileveled understanding of oppression and then act upon it.

In SPD, through participation in courses, workshops, and other activities, students acquire the "knowledge, analytical skills, emotional faculties, and the capacity for action in political and social systems necessary to interpret and resist oppression" (Watts et al., 2003, p. 185). The stages of SPD theory trace a process in which students' development of critical consciousness leads to ultimate involvement in liberatory actions. Freire (1970, 1972) describes critical consciousness as the process by which students achieve a deepening awareness both of the sociocultural reality that shapes their lives and of their capacity to transform that reality. Critical consciousness not only involves a new understanding or critique of social and educational inequality but also entails a necessity for some sort of action to be taken to address the inequity (Freire, 1972; Tunstall, 2011; Watts et al., 2003). SPD involves the juxtaposition of theory and action where students gain knowledge and perspective on the role of oppression in their lives and educational experience, and then organize to address inequities within their community and school.

Within SJYD and SPD, adults are central to students' development process. SJYD understands the importance of schools, parents, and adults in providing supportive contexts in which youth can thrive (Benson & Scales, 2009; Ginwright & James, 2002; Lerner et al., 2005). Parents and educators working collectively with youth to develop critical consciousness and take social action is a pillar of SJYD (Ginwright & James, 2002). Similarly, SPD theory involves educators helping students to "recognize, understand and critique current social inequalities" (Ladson-Billings, 1995, p. 476). Practitioners and instructors within the VIPS program use SPD to effectively move students through a process whereby they learn to challenge multiple forms of oppression through their development of critical consciousness leading to critical action. Critical action follows the development of critical consciousness and describes the specific actions students engage in within their school or community for the expressed purpose of addressing social and educational inequalities (Tunstall, 2011). With these outcomes, youth demonstrate praxis by moving from learning and analysis to action that benefits not only them but also their communities and larger political structures.

VIPS AND SOCIAL JUSTICE YOUTH DEVELOPMENT AND SOCIOPOLITICAL DEVELOPMENT

The purpose of VIP Scholars is to develop competitive African American college applicants while engaging them in praxis in order to analyze the circumstances affecting the state of African American educational and social achievement. To that end, the program seeks to build a viable pipeline of competitively eligible students in schools that it works with that can lead to greater access to prestigious universities locally and nationally. Moreover, the goal would be to provide additional college preparation supports to frequently underresourced local high schools to assist students in postsecondary pursuits. This is done through the enactment of pedagogy of change that centers students' experiences in the program design. Students are pushed to take action after becoming more critically conscious of the economic, historical, political, educational, and social disparities many African Americans face. The program reflects SJYD and SPD principles and practices, with its intentional focus on social justice and developing critical consciousness in its participants. These elements are reflected in courses, reading material, workshops, staff training, and fieldtrips and even in movies that students watch and analyze. In VIPS, students participate in praxis through critical pedagogy and collective action guided by strong youth–adult relationships.

VIPS Program—Theory in Action

The VIPS summer program is most demonstrative of the SJYD and SPD models. Undergraduate mentors recruit high school students during the latters' sophomore year for the program's summer component. By the time of application, students must have a minimum 3.0 GPA in order to apply, as that is the minimum requirement for University of California applicants. The GPA requirement is adjusted for students demonstrating high potential and living in particularly stressful contexts. In doing so, VIPS acknowledges the various social environments that contribute to students' levels of academic achievement and insist that these youth still possess valuable assets (Ginwright & Cammarota, 2002; Lerner et al., 2005). Many students who are not accepted as summer program participants still receive ongoing mentoring and join the program's Saturday Academy component and can therefore still benefit from the social justice and college information workshops, family activities, and collective action.

Students who are accepted into the summer program spend two consecutive summers living in university campus dormitories while taking various courses. Undergraduate mentors and senior adults serving as program coordinators live with the youth in the residence halls. The residential aspect of the program encourages collective action by all parties in the program as they live, learn, and work together to build community among themselves while strategizing steps in courses or small groups for mobilizing against oppressive structures (Ginwright & James, 2002). Students are taught lessons of group accountability, in that they must all work together to ensure that each student follows rules and completes assignments. The residential aspect also creates a safe space for students, where gender-neutral language is encouraged and offensive language is prohibited, allowing students to celebrate their own unique identities and discuss sensitive topics (Ginwright & James, 2002; Terry et al., 2014).

The 1st year of the summer component consists of four major courses and activities: SAT preparation course, critical writing course, community-building activities, and bus trip analysis. Each of these components is chosen for various reasons. The SAT preparation and writing courses are important because of the need to strengthen students' test-taking and writing skills, which are vital for college admission. The community-building activities are designed to help students develop a sense of academic camaraderie that is essential to their time together in the program, where group accountability and support is expected. The bus trip entails an expedition through local Los Angeles communities to examine demographic changes, different socioeconomic areas of the city, and other observations. The 2nd year focuses mainly on Education 98—an undergraduate education course that analyzes race, class, and gender in the context of educational inequalities—a Fiat Lux, "let there be light," seminar focused on student activism and social movements, and a University of California admissions course taught by UCLA admissions officers. During both summers, students critique films and documentaries, attend social justice workshops, participate in small-group projects, and plan for structured action within their schools through a VIPS club. Both the 2-week and 5-week programs happen concurrently, meaning that rising juniors and rising seniors live together during the summer program and therefore work together in creating their club plans and moving toward collective action. The entire model of the program, including courses and activities, is to create a learning experience encompassing critical pedagogy. Critical pedagogy fosters critical consciousness and social action in students as they analyze power structures and work toward liberation from oppressive constructs (Freire, 1970).

Social Justice Activities: Summer 1

During summer 1, students take a writing course intended to strengthen critical thinking and analysis through writing, reading, discussions, and presentations using culturally relevant material. Throughout the course, the instructor incorporates social justice themes through topics such as immigration, sex trafficking, economic access, literacy, and power, and uses literary selections from African American writers such as James Baldwin, Toni Morrison, and Octavia Butler to engage students. Students receive extensive feedback and engage in multiple rewrites. This class functions not only to improve students' writing skills but to also create awareness of and identification with African American cultural pride as a protective factor (Ginwright & James, 2002; Miller & MacIntosh, 1999). By engaging with this course, students are able to put African American experiences as expressed through literature in the context of White dominant power, leading to critical consciousness and helping to build resilience in students. Like all instructors who teach VIPS courses—with the exception of contracted SAT preparation and UC admissions courses—the writing teacher engages a style that reflects what Freire (1970) called problem posing, a dialogic teaching method that allows students to think critically about material and engage in discussions with teachers and fellow students. According to Freire (1970), this type of teaching leads to liberation through education and challenges traditional, authoritarian methods of teaching that position students as lacking assets and teachers as all-knowing. VIPS high school students are treated as college students as they meet one-on-one with instructors to speak bidirectionally about reading material and the critical writing process.

The 1st year of the summer program also includes a bus trip activity in which students take one public bus from the pristine environment of Beverly Hills to the south-central Los Angeles neighborhood of Leimert Park. Leimert Park was once booming with Black businesses, until the Los Angeles Uprisings of 1992 when racial tensions in the city led to the destruction of property in the area. In contrast to Beverly Hills, south-central Los Angeles is predominately African American and low income. Students ride the public bus through Los Angeles, taking note of the changes in property, demographics, businesses, and overall environment as they move from affluent Beverly Hills to Leimert Park. Many student participants who live in the Leimert Park area are moved to reflect on the inequality between their neighborhood and predominately White neighborhoods, allowing them to think critically about community and social problems (Ginwright & James, 2002). A key goal for the end of year 1 is that students identify key historical and contemporary factors that explain inequality and that they describe ways that education can play a key role in transforming such circumstances for them personally and for their families, schools, and communities.

Social Justice Activities: Summer 2

Students in the 2nd year participate in a 5-week residential program through which they enroll in a 4-unit undergraduate course, Education 98: Race, Class, and Inequalities in the United States, and engage intensively with college-level scholarship and write two analytical papers each week. This course provides students with a basis for understanding the educational experiences of underrepresented groups in U.S. public schools. Students also engage in discourse around larger social issues, such as the role schools play in the socialization of young people and as instruments of social control and stratification. Through this course of study, students work with the instructors to consider ways in which the problems facing U.S. schools can be more effectively remedied. Students also take a one-unit seminar course focused on community empowerment. These courses educate students on social inequalities and allow them to reflect on how they affect their lives (Ginwright & James, 2002).

In the Education 98 course, the instructor and teaching assistants engage students in problem-posing teaching practices, presenting ideas to students and asking them to critically discuss topics (Freire, 1970). Class is structured as a dialogic space in which the student voice is just as important as that of the teacher. After reading texts that examine education practices that create unequal opportunities for people of different races, classes, and genders, students write reflective journals, in which they reflect on the material, pose questions, and write about the topics in the context of their experiences. This way of learning and engaging with course material is the first step in becoming critically conscious before moving to social action and liberation (Freire, 1970; Ginwright & James, 2002). The culminating project for the education course is a research paper in which students identify the resources available to them at their high schools in comparison to more affluent high schools in Los Angeles. Students use the comparison to argue for reasons why the majority of African American and Latino students are not college ready or matriculating into selective universities at the rates of students from other racial groups.

The Fiat Lux course is the most action-oriented course, one that specifically aims to equip students with the knowledge, attitude, and skills essential to students becoming vibrant agents of social change. In this seminar revolving around varying topics, students engage in discussions about historical and current issues that affect people of color and ways to create change. For example, the summer 2014 Fiat Lux course was called "Critical Media Literacy: Social Justice and Student Activism." Not only did students critically examine media images of African Americans and Latinos and representations of current social issues, but they also thought about how media could be used for positive social change. Students worked in groups to create nonprofit proposals to solve a specific issue in the Black community using social media networks and mass media to spread awareness and attract participants and stakeholders to the cause. In this instance, students move from critical consciousness to action, particularly collective action, by seeking to create social and systemic change (Tunstall, 2011). As students learn about social issues they become invested in fighting injustice they experience in their lives and see in their communities and are motivated by their voices being valued (Larson et al., 2005; Pearce, 2007). The goals of the 2nd year are that students have completed the majority of their UC applications, completed a "brag sheet" of their leadership and other extracurricular activities since they have been in high school, and improved their research and writing skills. Secondary goals are to have compiled a list of colleges students will apply to, identified potential letter writers for their college applications (where applicable), and described their goals for their senior years in high school.

Student Action and Adults

The SJYD and SPD goal of moving from critical consciousness to social action works best when adults support students (Ginwright & James, 2002). Adults in VIPS fulfill many roles as UCLA staff and faculty. Their expertise, research, and networks all contribute to the development of social capital among VIPS students as adults connect youth with resources and assist them in the development of their own research and action initiatives (Jarrett et al., 2005). As VIPS students seek to share the information they acquire through the summer program and move to action, adults support them in creating functioning VIPS clubs at their respective high schools.

VIPS clubs provide a schoolwide opportunity for VIPS students to further develop as leaders and advocates for social justice. During the summer program, students meet with other students from their high schools—both rising juniors and rising seniors—and with VIPS adults to identify issues at their respective campuses and within their communities that they want to actively change. The clubs are student run but undergraduate mentors support the students in any way possible to facilitate the expressed goals of the club. Under this design, mentors scaffold to help provide structure and use their resources to provide necessary connections to stakeholders and authorities in order to successfully create change (Larson et al., 2005). Scaffolding allows students to effectively collaborate with adults and also to build their own leadership skills and sense of agency (Zeldin, 2004). For example, a group of VIPS students who experienced racial discrimination at UCLA collaborated with VIPS staff to meet with members of the university administration, who were then prompted to create an online bias-reporting platform specifically for issues of tolerance. Another student took her summer research project, which outlined her school's lack of resources compared with those of a more affluent school, and used the VIPS club as a platform to hold a community forum at her high school with community political leaders and school board members, resulting in the donation of brand-new textbooks and a redesigned computer lab; the computer lab at the school is now named after that student. Other students have started VIPS clubs that organized college visits and cultural fieldtrips, while others implemented mentoring programs between upperclassmen and lowerclassmen as a way of addressing the poor retention rate of African American students at the high schools. Adults help to foster leadership in VIPS students, who then use their critical consciousness to move to action at their schools with other students, engaging in collective action. VIPS students understand that it is their duty as conscious individuals to share their knowledge with other members of their community in order to enact change. Allowing youth to have governance roles is beneficial to their development of agency and competency and adds value to the entire programs and adult knowledge of effectively working with youth (Zeldin, 2004).

VIPS Saturday Academies provide another space for students and their families to engage in social justice and college information workshops geared toward collective action. Upon acceptance into VIPS, students attend their first Saturday Academy with their parents/guardian. It is here that VIPS staff begin with contextualizing issues facing African American and other underrepresented students. They begin the process of analyzing power in social relationships and identify how to participate in collective action toward change (Ginwright & James, 2002). Saturday Academies are quarterly meetings for VIPS students and families. During the meetings, students and families spend a Saturday at UCLA learning about social justice issues, college preparation strategies, and building a coalition of students, parents, and VIPS undergraduate mentors. Youth benefit greatly from participating in shared activities with their parents (Hamilton & Hamilton, 2004). In particular, Jarrett (1995) argues that families aid African American youth in overcoming obstacles thrown up by oppressive environments through specific practices including a "supportive adult network structure" and "strategic alliances with mobility enhancing institutions and organizations," (p. 114). Further, African American youth in families that engage in cognitive reframing and problem solving in response to discrimination by reaching out to others within the Black community are more likely to have a positive racial identity (Townsend & Lanphier, 2007). Families work to offset possible negative impacts of racism and systems of social inequality in maintaining high self-esteem among Black youth (Hughes & Demo, 1989). Thus, in working together, VIPS staff, students, and their families learn about and organize for social action during Saturday Academies.

We believe VIPS is effective because of its work to not only prepare students for college but also empower them to become agents of change. Becoming agents of change has manifested in many ways. Not only have students gone to and completed college (for many, as the first in their families) but many have volunteered or worked at their local high schools to assist students with the college prep process. Others have taken on leadership roles in their respective colleges, dedicated to equity and access for underserved communities. Another area where students have committed to becoming change agents has been in the majors and career fields they have selected. Many of the students have chosen pre-law or pre-medicine or social welfare, education, or psychology major and career path. It should be noted that alumni data collected from VIP Scholars are replete with students changing the narrative on urban youth by receiving awards, accolades, and recognition at their respective colleges and demonstrating what is possible for students when given the appropriate supports. Within the VIP Scholars program, just as it is expected that student participants will perform well in school and attend selective colleges and universities, it is expected that students will engage in their home, school, and communities in meaningful ways to address social justice issues that affect their daily lived experiences.

Three

Mentorship and Mentoring

Tyrone C. Howard and Bree Blades

An integral, and arguably the most fundamental, aspect of the VIP Scholars program is mentoring. Though not identified at the outset of the program design as a primary objective for college-going urban youth, the influence of faculty, staff, and college students on the high school students undoubtedly over time became one of the program's biggest strengths. A plethora of works has documented the importance of mentoring as a key component in youth development (Grossman & Tierney, 1998; Rhodes & DuBois, 2007; Rhodes & Lowe, 2008; Crisp & Cruz, 2009). Much of the literature on mentorship has described it as a more seasoned, experienced, and informed individual providing guidance, assistance, concern, and care for either younger or more inexperienced individuals (DuBois & Karcher, 2005). Others have described mentoring as an apprenticeship, with one person providing knowledge and skills to another person (Herrera, Grossmen, Kauh, & McMaken, 2011). Philip (2000) states that the definition of youth mentoring is "an older experienced guide who is acceptable to the young person and who can help ease the transition to adulthood by a mix of support and challenge" (p. 12). Another important feature of mentorship is the idea of demonstrating a set way of knowing, doing, and comprehending a particular task or defined goal. In this chapter we will explore the salience of mentoring in the VIP Scholars program. In doing so, we have four key objectives. First, we will highlight and define the various aspects of mentoring as defined in the professional literature. Second, we will discuss how mentoring played out in the VIPS program, with a particular focus on student voices and descriptions of mentoring. It should be noted that the mentorship demonstrated throughout the program was multilayered and went beyond academics, which is why for the third objective we will use data from the students to articulate and highlight the different types of mentorship that were provided in the program. This section of the chapter will center on academic, social, emotional, and personal mentorship. Finally, we will conclude the chapter with a set of recommendations for mentorship arrangements in college outreach programs based on what we have learned from 10 years of work with youth from urban schools and communities.

DEFINING MENTORSHIP

In short, being a mentor is assisting others in the acquisition of the essential knowledge, skills, and dispositions to master a particular goal (Ahn, 2010; Daloz, 1999; Kram, 1985; Rhodes, 2002). Blackwell (1989) describes mentoring as a relationship in which one is being tied to "a person of superior rank, special achievements, and prestige" (p. 9). This person often serves in a protective role and works with his or her protégé to ensure that the latter avoids mistakes, pitfalls, and setbacks that may be common in a particular journey. The professional literature typically describes mentoring as a process that entails an intense dyadic relationship in which the mentor furthers the professional and personal development of the protégé, providing information, assistance, support, and guidance around supportive activities by observing, demonstrating, providing feedback, and working collaboratively toward the mentee's proficiency in various tasks (Keller, 2005).

Sipe (1998) synthesized the literature on youth mentoring and concluded that successful mentors tended to be a steady and involved presence in the youth's lives, respecting the youth's viewpoints, and seeking supervision from support staff when needed. Other scholars have discussed the value of mentoring where issues of social, professional, and personal matters are concerned. Rhodes (2002), for example, has stated that there is an extensive number of mentoring programs and that they vary in scope, function, and purpose. However, her theoretical framing on mentoring suggests that effective mentoring must have four key components—interpersonal connections, mutuality, empathy, and trust—to be most effective. The interview data from VIP Scholars were consistently clear that the students benefited from the type of mentorship that was tied to each of these characteristics. Throughout this chapter we will lay out the descriptors that students offered about how the mentoring they received benefited them personally and academically.

Mentoring in the context of VIP Scholars was centered not only on college preparation but also on personal development, community improvement, and academic excellence, along with the development of a critical consciousness, as discussed in the previous chapter. Thus, mentoring was not merely a professional pairing of mentor and mentee; rather, these arrangements formed organically across different spaces with different types of mentors. The level of mentorship was multitiered as well. This often meant program mentors (who were undergraduate students) mentored high school students, teaching assistants (who were graduate students) mentored undergraduate students and high school students, and faculty and staff in the program mentored teaching assistants. The intricacy of this mentorship pipeline is further explained in the following chapter.

At the core of the mentorship practices displayed within the program were investment in time, imparting of knowledge, skills, and operating from the belief and practice that students had the aptitude to be college eligible, succeed in college, and become a change agent in their school and community. Perhaps most critical to the various mentoring arrangements that were present in the program was a fundamental belief in the potential of each of the high school students to become college students. The belief in the students' academic and professional potential was expressed early and then often throughout the program. The strong sentiment of high expectations was put best by a rising VIPS senior, who stated, "It makes a big difference when everybody is just expecting you to go to college. You just start believing and acting that way."

Another unique feature of VIP Scholars that we address in other parts of this book is that while many college preparatory programs center on solely getting students into college, VIPS was also committed to helping students develop a critical consciousness about inequities in schools and communities. Tunstall (2011) describes the development of this critical consciousness as a process that "enables students to become conscious of and gain a greater perspective on their social reality and of themselves, thereby mobilizing them to engage in a process of reflection and action to change the reality" (p. 67). The program was also focused on assisting students to successfully matriculate through college to graduation within a 4- to 5-year window. Therefore, mentorship here again was multifaceted and not tied to a unitary goal of getting students into college but to working with students to help them develop a sense of self and identifying ways to improve their school and community and to see successful matriculation through college as part of becoming a change agent. Figure 3.1 outlines the manner in which three core foci were the ways that mentorship occurred within the VIPS program.

Multilayered mentoring is critical because it is often contextual and looks different for different students and communities. Therefore, it is vitally important to document what mentoring looks like in the high-school-to-college transition process for students of color in low-income communities. Tierney, Bailey, Constantine, Finkelstein, and Hurd (2009) argue that high schools must establish a "culture of achievement" if young people, especially

Figure 3.1. Three Key Foci of VIPS Mentorship

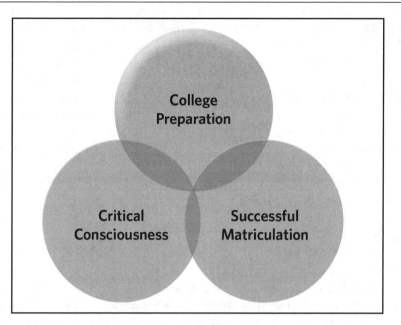

those from historically marginalized culture groups, are to be prepared for college-level work (p. 9). What became evident in working with students from the VIP Scholars program was that many of them did not come from high schools where a culture of achievement, or high expectations for college attainment, was evident. For most of the schools, VIPS partners with the number of students who attended 4-year universities was typically below 10%, and the number who attended more selective and prestigious universities directly out of high school was below 5%. These numbers are not too different for many urban schools across the nation, thus making the importance of mentoring even more salient. The mentoring that took place in the VIP Scholars program was centered on the creation of a "culture of high achievement" that was demonstrated by program staff daily. Tierney (2009) states that schools that maintain high expectations for academic achievement and pay close attention to the student behaviors and habits that predict college readiness are the most successful in creating this culture of high achievement. He asserts that these are also schools that likely have multiple instructional and social supports for students as they progress from the freshmen to senior year of high school. Much of what the VIP Scholars program sought to do was to establish a culture of high achievement, but also appropriate social and emotional supports. This culture was most embodied by the UCLA students who served as mentors in the program. As referred to earlier, these students represented a wide range of majors, from pre-medicine, psychology, philosophy, pre-law, economics, and history. Student mentors would frequently study with the high school students, discuss effective study skills, read drafts of papers, describe steps needed to be successful in college, and talk about the importance of time management and discipline, serving overall as role models for aspiring college students. What the data will also highlight in this chapter is the way that mentorship was not only academic; it also focused on personal hardships, social and emotional difficulties, and life challenges in general. Perhaps most crucial to the mentor–mentee relationship was the fact that many of the UCLA undergraduate mentors attended the same schools or were from the same or similar communities as the mentees. This resulted in a level of connectedness and familiarity with cultural context that provided mentors the ability to know and understand the challenges that mentees face where issues of school, community, family, and life were concerned.

An additional aspect of the mentoring in the VIP Scholars program was that during the summer programs, mentors lived in the dormitories, as the students did; accompanied them to and sat in on classes; and oversaw the various academic tasks that students were expected to complete. Thus, the mentors had an informed view of the academic, personal, and social dynamics that were occurring with the students while they were in the program. It should also be noted that racial/ethnic and community matches between mentor and mentees are helpful in the relationship, but by no means are they vital for an effective mentoring relationship to occur. All the mentors in the program were either Latino or African American. Some scholars have questioned whether traditional mentoring arrangements (largely White male to White male) have applicability for women and people of color. There have been few systematic examinations of the effect of the race/ethnicity and gender of mentors on the trajectories of people of color and their inclusion or exclusion from disciplinary networks (Bonilla-Silva 2011; Lee, 1999; Turner, Myers, & Cresswell 1999). However, there has been a call for more "cultural competency" in mentoring (Davidson & Foster-Johnson 2001; Wilson-Ahlstrom, Ravindranath, Yohalem, & Tseng 2010). The idea of cultural competency in mentoring is tied to having a knowledge of, respect for, and understanding of the cultural knowledge and experiences of mentees. This is important because of the unique experiences of people of color and individuals from low-income backgrounds.

Connected to the salience of cultural competence is the ability to relate to and support the academic and emotional needs of historically marginalized student groups. A growing body of research has examined the effectiveness of mentorship on historically marginalized groups. For example, Laden (1999) used qualitative methods to address the needs of first-generation Latino community college students in California. The Puente Project provided a model to foster and socialize historically "at risk" students as they matriculate into a bachelor degree–granting institution. The participants received an abundance of cultural affirmation, community cultural wealth, and mentorship about organizational socialization. Although the study examined the experiences of Latino community college students, the information shared is relevant here, because the findings demonstrate that mentoring is a critical element of the Puente Project, since the volunteers are seen as cultural role models, which provide a counternarrative to the dominant discourse. Ahn (2010) studied the role of social networks on mentors and how the latter's social capital affects their mentees' college-going process. The research concerned a college-mentoring program affiliated with a large urban university. The study operated under a network-analytic and social capital framework to understand how network location can affect mentoring programs. The findings reveal that networking could be one of the most invaluable aspects of mentorship; connecting mentees to people, resources, and relevant services is critical to success in any endeavor. This work is relevant to mentorship in the VIPS context because it examines what spaces and networks mentors use to provide resources for mentees. Moreover, the CollegeMentor program that Ahn (2010) discusses can help us understand how programs can collaborate to effectively maximize networks to increase college access for underserved populations. Finally, other scholars have talked about the manner in which mentoring within educational contexts is more effective when it is holistic in approach and scope (Laden, 1999; Tierney, 2009).

ACADEMIC MENTORSHIP

Throughout the interview and focus group data that we collected it was clear that according to the students, the most essential mentoring was done through academic and social–emotional supports. In the following section, we will discuss both areas and identify data points where students talked about the benefits of both types of mentorship. Given that VIP Scholars is a program with an explicit focus on increasing students' competitiveness for college admission, it came as no surprise that the students repeatedly mentioned how much they gained from learning about the particulars of getting into college and how much the mentors in the program demystified the process for them. The overwhelming majority of the students were the first in their families who would be attending university, so they talked about "not having anyone at home to help me" in the college pursuit. Many of the students stated that their high schools did a poor job of preparing them for college or that there was a sole focus on high school graduation, and postsecondary education was neglected. While a number of the students were able to talk with teachers at their schools or find fleeting moments with school counselors, the point was clear that most of the students believed that they were "on our own" where college preparation was concerned. As a result, the desire to go to college, which all the students possessed, and the structures to support that pursuit were largely incongruent. Hence, the students talked about the relief and absolute satisfaction they felt in having structured and consistent access to people who were dedicated to their college pursuit through the VIPS program. The students were consistent in their belief that the program helped to uncover the hidden curriculum or the unknown aspects of applying to and getting into college. Darius talked about this reality when he commented:

> VIPS has shined the light on everything that was hidden. I know more about college now, and I feel more empowered and also like it's not just based on academics; it's also like a family-type environment and so I feel comfortable opening up to people.

Students also talked about the value of consistently being informed and reminded about the types of courses that they needed to be taking and performing well in to get into the college of their choice. The students frequently mentioned how simple, yet transformative, it was to have this type of information. Khalifah talked about what she gained from her mentorship:

> I think this was more of a life lesson, because we were like taking these classes, getting a perspective on like how the future is gonna be for us in college and everything. But then you know like I kinda thought about it last night like when you have like our mentors who are also spending all day with us and they stay up till after 11 like after bed check doing our meetings and stuff, and then Whitney having a midterm like last Wednesday or Thursday. They do a lot.

The students talked increasingly about how hearing the testimonies of the mentors helped them to realize that college students also struggled with doubt, frustration, insecurity, lack of academic preparation, and the need for sheer persistence just as they did in high school. Kenya stated:

> Tre'Vel told us this story yesterday about how he like just never gives up and he told us stuff that happened to him [in college] and then it's like a life lesson because like we get to share all these things about ourselves with each other.

The students discussed how mentorship was important in their preparation for college, especially when it came from undergraduate students who knew about the process. And several talked about this reality:

> I've established numerous relationships with my mentors, my peers, as well as the teachers that were there for us, and I feel like after this program I felt way more prepared than I was and I learned a lot of things I did not know was necessary for entering college. —Kenyon (rising 12th-grader)

There were consistent words of gratitude offered by the students to the mentors about their investment into their overall pursuit of college.

> I wanted to kind of thank the mentors because they did give us options when plans didn't go as scheduled. They came telling us over and over about the importance of classes, what to take, what not to take. It was like having a real college counselor. —Jaxon (rising 12th-grader)

The idea of pushing the students to higher academic levels came up repeatedly from the students. Several of the high school students discussed always being at the top of the class, being the smartest students in class, and feeling as if they knew what it took to be good students. However, upon spending time with the mentors during the summer program, the students learned that they needed to be, and could be, pushed more academically to be even better. Sha'Vonna stated:

> You know, you think you are a hard worker, and you have everything down, but then you see your mentors, working full time, and then studying until 3 in the morning, it makes you realize "man, they work really hard."

Another student, Terah commented that perhaps the most critical takeaway she received from the program was just observing the mentors and how hard they worked on their own classes, while also working in the program:

> It's not so much what the mentors said, you know. I mean, that was important, but watching them was it for me. They studied a lot, had flashcards, took these hard classes, and were just really focused. That showed me what it means to be a college student.

Some students confided that they struggled with certain areas academically, but they felt comfortable discussing this with their mentors, and how they improved as a result. Indigo said:

I've improved my writing since I've been here because I was horrible, I'm tellin' you I was horrible with my writing . . . but now like with our mentors they helped us so much that when you go back to school you're not gonna be better than everyone, but you gonna have like a little piece of you that says, "oh, I think you should do this, I think you should do that." My writing is much better because of VIPS and my mentors.

It should be noted that mentoring has a cultural context to it that is crucial. A number of scholars have discussed how culture and care merge in unique ways for different people (Howard, 2010; Valenzuela, 1999). While the students were effusive in their praise of the mentors, they did discuss how often the care shown toward them was manifested through "tough love" or being "hard on us." The types of descriptions of mentoring described by some of the students are in line with what Kleinfeld (1975) described as "warm demanders." Kleinfeld (1975) coined this phrase to describe the type of teacher who was effective in teaching Athabaskan Indian and Eskimo 9th-graders in Alaskan schools. These teachers communicated personal warmth and used an instructional style Kleinfeld called "active demandingness." At least one of the students from the program, Theda, gave an account of how this type of support was instrumental in her academic success:

The mentors are like great . . . even though sometimes they're like mean and stuff they just wanna help you. . . . They are hard on you but in a good way. They have the utmost care for you and like they just want you to do better. You just have to remember that when they are pushing you as much as they do sometime.

The value of mentoring within a cultural context cannot be overstated. Much has been written about the complexity of culture (Howard, 2010). Germane to the concept of culture are the types of knowledge, values, and ways of communication that are relevant to a particular group of people. Cultural knowledge, as Erickson (2012) reminds us,

begins through child rearing and continued through further socialization throughout the life span. . . . Human *culture* is intrinsically connected with human education, formal and informal. It can be thought of as the basic "curriculum" of any social group; the patterns of organization within conduct of everyday life. (p. 560)

It is an understanding of the "basic curriculum" that the mentors seemed to understand most about the students. It should be noted that culture here is not discussed in an essentialized way, as if all the students shared and had the same cultural knowledge and skills. Although all students were African American and Latino, the mentors recognized the differences that existed within and across racial and ethnic groups. Mentors learned more about this cultural knowledge of the students by spending time with them, learning about them, and querying them about their families, schools, communities, ambitions, likes, and dislikes. Given the type of connectedness that existed between the students and mentors, the ability of the mentors to know whom, how, and when to push students and challenge them to do better is critical here. Moreover, for the students to not misinterpret these efforts is also important. This type of unending encouragement, support, and pushing was not lost on the students. Tendai offered the following sentiment:

> I remember the first day we had to finish like uh, two and a half pages on research papers within like 2 days. They were hard on us, pushing us, telling us to get it done. But it helped. . . . I was like "how am I gonna do this?" This is like our first day, why are they assigning all this work? And then like our mentors and just like everyone was like "oh, you can do this," like giving you help, and now like I'm just like "oh, okay, I can do this research paper."

The types of skills that the students gained from their mentors seem to have utility beyond the program; students mentioned that they "learned how to study like college students" and felt stronger as students going back to their senior year of high school after being challenged academically. Others even talked about how they would help their peers who were not in the program. Brandi said:

> I feel like they [the mentors] really like show you how to be a good student. . . . I mean, like you can even take this back home and give support to your friends 'cause you know that it is so effective.

Perhaps the most poignant descriptor of the value of mentorship in the program was offered by Indigo:

> I learned that there, how do I word this . . . like there's so many things as an African American person that sets us back, we have to prove all these people wrong here. . . . Like the mentors here, they're proving everybody wrong by being in these classes, graduating and stuff, and I feel like I need to prove these people wrong too. And they have been good role models. . . . Even though my parents didn't go to college . . . I can still

be a scholar, I can still go to college, and I feel like that's gonna help me so much, when I feel like I can't do things in high school, I'm a be like "remember that program, remember the mentors, remember what these other kids have to go through that's even worse than mine," like my struggles, and it's gonna help me like persevere.

MENTORING: SOCIAL AND EMOTIONAL

One of the important aspects of mentoring within the context of the VIPS framework that was ideal for students of color in low-income communities is the importance of social and emotional support. While it is important to provide skills and assistance in the technical aspects of the academic work and tasks, it is also crucial to be able to support students socially and emotionally, as this can have a direct impact on their ability to perform academically. A growing body of literature has focused on the salience of social and emotional learning as a means to engage students in a learning process that recognizes the complexities and challenges of living and learning. The Collaborative for Academic, Social, and Emotional Learning (CASEL) (2014) states:

> Social emotional learning is based on the understanding that the best learning emerges in the context of supportive relationships that make learning challenging, engaging and meaningful.

The idea put forth by CASEL is tied to five core competencies:

- Self-management
- Self-awareness
- Social awareness
- Responsible decisionmaking
- Relationship skills

India discussed the social and emotional support she received from one of her mentors:

> She [Sandra] was strict but she wasn't strict to the point where it's like you just can't even talk to her. She did her job, but she did her job to an extent. Like, you were able to talk to her; you were able to have a conversation with her. She let you do your own thing but she still abided by the rules.

The importance of the social and emotional needs of students was not lost on many of the high school students. It is crucial to note that, much like other students from urban communities, many of the students in the program faced myriad personal, social, familial, and financial challenges. Scholars have discussed the need for school settings to be more aware and supportive of the obstacles that students face in their daily lives (Duncan-Andrade, 2005; Valenzuela, 1999). The interview data were full of various accounts in which the students talked continually about the mentors' ability to "care" or "show concern" for them beyond just preparing for college or their academic pursuits. A number of the students in the program were foster youth and faced challenges with their living arrangements and family circumstances; other students had extremely difficult relationships with their parents that caused challenges. Nonetheless, despite these real-life trials the students felt as though their mentors in the program did not judge them or look at them differently because of these situations. Jackson commented:

> I love how the mentors know that we have real-life stuff going on, and they listen to you and still support you. I would never share some of the things with teachers at my school, like I shared with the mentors. They can just relate on a lot of levels.

The ability to "relate on a lot of levels" was repeated often. Central to the importance of the mentor–mentee relationship was the fact many of the mentors were products of the same communities, schools, and circumstances as the mentees. This proved to be valuable in the mentor–mentee relationship because not only were mentors able to empathize with some of the life challenges that the students faced, but also many of the mentors had gone through similar situations themselves and, perhaps most important, were able to help the students problem solve or acquire the skills or resources to address the challenges that they faced. Rickie, a rising junior, commented:

> I just want to thank the mentors, especially Whitney, for not giving up on me when I was going through some tough times at home. She talked about things that she had been through, and it make me feel like, "okay, I can get through this." And she always checked in on me to make sure I was okay. I loved her for that.

Throughout the interviews conducted with students, comments such as "VIPS is like a community" or "VIPS is like a family to me" were frequently made. A number of students discussed how the level of mentorship that they received helped erase their doubts and fears about going to college. As Jacqueline discussed:

> VIPS is a place where I feel like um I can be open to people, that I'm not usually open to like as far as schooling and home. I guess you could say it's an opportunity to learn different techniques of how to approach schooling.

The relatability factor was significant and was referred to consistently by the students. Words like *connect, relate, understanding,* and *care* were frequently used. Lucious, for example, talked about the value of connecting with his mentors:

> I love how you can really open up to these mentors and you can really have a good bond with them like um and as far as the workshops go these workshops they really taught us some life lessons and then were right there when we're doing these workshops. At first we think it's fun and games but as we sit down and discuss it we're really like sitting there and were really going over it and were really seeing like wow all that you're saying here really incorporates with what we're doing and I just like how we can have that special bond with the mentor.

With the recognition that students bring a wealth of personal and familial issues to these academic spaces, it is critical to note that the training for the mentors included training from both counselors and psychologists about how to address, respond to, or support the students when it came to nonacademic issues. As important as providing mentors with effective training is identifying, recruiting, and hiring UCLA undergraduate students who were either first-generation college students, students of color, graduates of low-income urban schools, or products of such communities. Seemingly inherent in many of these students' background was knowing firsthand the types of social and emotional needs that students need in the pursuit of academic success. One of the mentors from the program talked about this:

> I know for me, it's not just about the academics; it's about all the other drama you have in your life. Dealing with family issues, not having money, just struggling. So when the scholars talk about it, I can relate, and so can a lot of the other mentors. That's what makes VIPS special; we are all in this together.

The students discussed the types of relationships that were established as a result of these connections. One high school student commented:

I actually formed some bonds with them [the mentors] like I understand them and they understand me and I know whatever they do is beneficial for us and it's not just to bring us down or anything like that.

Another student commented about the directors of the program, who also were mentors and vital to the program's success:

Jonli and Jerry are like really, really good mentors because they were supportive and they were like . . . they were just a really good support factor for us and they helped us through a lot and it was definitely like we did create close bonds with them and we could talk them about a whole bunch of stuff. So it was just it was good to have them in our cohort and like to expand these views and I know I wanna go to UCLA so it was good to come here and experience this.

It was also evident, according to the students, that often their academic success is tied directly to their social and emotional state. Astin provided a cogent example:

See, what teachers in school don't understand is that when things in your life are not right, you don't care about a class, an assignment, or even school that much. Here the mentors got that. . . . If you can help me or at least understand my life stuff, then you also can help me academically, because all that stuff is—how do you say it—interconnected.

Consistently across the data as the students were asked to comment on the quality of the mentors and how they did or did not assist them, students were excessive in their praise. Bri stated:

I think the whole mentor thing . . . they're doing good with that. Cuz like I love all the mentors, not only that but I felt a connection with them, and like they can like relate to us. And sometimes they'd get down and be serious, like . . . and they understand we're gonna be up till like 4 in the morning. But, so, I mean I love the mentors, 'cause like they really connect with us, and also push us to, to take advantage of where we are.

Daisha mentioned how the mentors were instrumental in helping her come out of her shell socially, which was hard for her to do:

People may not really think this about me because they all say I'm funny for whatever reason but I'm actually kinda shy to talk to people. So like, since I feel like the mentors actually made you get to know people. I thought that had an impact on me to get to meet new people.

A.J. talked about how much the directors were a big help for him:

> I just wanna say thank you, I just wanted to thank like all of our mentors and Jonli and Jerry especially for helping us out. It's good to know that somebody actually does care about our education and that we have ways to improve where we're weak in different subjects at school. But to also have people who care about you as a person too. Yeah.

To stress the various types of mentorship, Morrow and Styles (1995) conducted interviews with more than 200 adolescents and found that mentoring relationships tended to fall into two broad categories, *developmental* and *prescriptive*. Satisfied pairs—defined by feelings of liking, attachment to, and commonality with the other members—were determined to be more developmental and youth-driven. Developmental pairs were considered reliable and trusting and enjoyable, and youth felt supported rather than judged. Prescriptive pairs, on the other hand, were characterized by adult-governed goals, no adjustment of expectations on the part of the adult, and a lack of consistent support from the adult. To stress this point, one of the students in the program expressed surprise at the type of support that she received from mentors that seemed to be more developmental, while she expected something more along the lines of a prescriptive approach:

> When I think of mentors, the first thing that comes to my mind is older people who are more detached from us, who we probably won't get along with, who are just there to just make sure we're doing what we're supposed to be doing, but these mentors are not that far away from us age-wise and they relate to us so they're easy to talk to.

Another student talked about the manner in which mentoring can be more effective when there is a relational component to it:

> Yeah, it was cool to kind of like have mentors, some who are still in college like going through, and like going through it, and like they went through what we're going through right now. Like it's a good experience.

Through the process of socialization, mentoring, and affiliation with peers there can be a multitude of impacts for youth in different positive (and negative) behaviors. Recent evidence suggests links to prosocial behaviors (e.g., volunteer work, academic activities), as well as health-promoting behaviors, such as exercise and fitness-related behaviors (Prinstein & Dodge, 2008). The responses from the VIP Scholars suggest that adolescents conform their behavior to perceived social norms in order to align with a desired group of peers (Dishion, Poulin, & Burraston, 2001). Those most likely to conform are often uncertain about aspects of their own self-identity, a process that typically heightens during times of school transitions. Conformity also increases when youth are around others of a perceived higher status and their affiliation comes with perceived social rewards (Cohen & Prinstein, 2006).

CONCLUSION

In short, mentorship matters. The idea of providing hands-on, caring, and informed guidance is crucial to the personal and academic success of young people, no matter what the goal may be. The scholars in the VIPS program were benefactors of an intense and sustained type of mentorship that many still recall years after they completed the program. The challenge that schools and universities face is how they can duplicate such mentorship arrangements in a manner that not only is driven by various individuals but also is an in-grained part of the structure of an educational program. In many ways, students are asking and looking for informed, caring, and concerned individuals who will invest in them without judging them or their personal lives and circumstances. Moreover, according to the data from the scholars in VIPS, this investment in them was invaluable. This investment led many of the scholars to then play a mentoring role at their schools with younger students, as well as leading many of the scholars to become mentors when they became college students. What we learn from this is that mentorship pays off in many ways and on many levels. Below, we provide recommendations for mentorship that may be considered for programs concerned with youth development.

- *Consistency.* In short, the ability to stay the course for the allotted time appears to have a significant influence on the quality and effectiveness of mentorship. Throughout our data students mentioned how much they could rely on mentors and their consistency in responding to the students' needs. Hence, the ability to provide steady and ongoing support is invaluable. Students talked about the inconsistency of people, resources, and support at respective schools and how much of a difference constancy made in their gaining access to college knowledge. Knowing that the mentor can be reliably reached, is timely, and is clear on follow-through of tasks is a must.

- *Relatedness.* Though this is not shown as a requirement in most of the literature on mentoring, the students in our program talked about the importance of having mentors who could relate to them socially, culturally, emotionally, and academically. Hence, it would seem that in order to identify effective mentors, it is essential to consider identifying individuals who have had similar circumstances to those of the prospective mentees. A strong academic profile and credentials alone do not make one an ideal mentor. Individuals who have dealt with life challenges and overcome adversity can offer insights that may not offered by higher-credentialed individuals. Factors that can help relatability may include having similar familial and social class backgrounds, school and academic experiences, or a familiarity with youth in these circumstances.

- *Whole-person development.* There is research on the multifaceted nature of mentorship. What was notable in this work was how mentors were able to support students holistically. Holistic mentorship is dedicated to a concern for the entire person. For the VIP Scholars program it was academic, social, emotional, and cultural modeling that all seemed to play a role in students' development. The importance of whole-person development does not negate the importance of mentorship in any one particular area, but it speaks to the manner in which connecting different parts of personal development can be helpful in multiple ways.

- *Mentorship training.* Mentorship is easier for some than for others. In that regard, it is important to note that any program concerned with providing mentorship with youth should consider the value of mentorship training. In these arrangements, mentors in training may role-play scenarios and how to appropriately respond and discuss potential situations that can arise with mentees, the limits of their support as mentors, and any potential downsides to building relationships with youth. They may read about different characteristics of mentoring, or they can reflect on and write about their own mentors and how they might replicate those behaviors. In short, the idea of having a structured way of discussing, defining, and demonstrating mentorship can go a long way in providing prospective mentors the skills and knowledge needed.

- *Competency matters.* Whatever the task that mentorship is being delivered in, it is absolutely mandatory that potential mentors have a high degree of competency in the goal that the mentee aspires to reach. Throughout our interviews with VIP Scholars, it was evident that the mentors in the program offered immediate credibility because they had been admitted to UCLA. Hence, they knew what was required to being accepted—certain courses, grades, SAT or ACT tests, extracurricular activities, and all the additional information required for being highly competitive for admission. Thus, however mentors are identified, perhaps the primary ingredient is a level of knowledge about the task that mentees aspire to achieve. Further training in these areas is also an important factor to increase mentors' knowledge base of academic requirements.

In conclusion, the importance of cross-age peer mentoring is important. Cross-age peer mentoring refers to a systematic approach to delivering mentoring services through the use of trained peers who are generally at least 2 years older than the mentees they serve (Karcher, 2013). Peer mentoring was quite evident in the VIPS program and fits into a larger category of youth mentoring, "structured and trusting relationships . . . with caring individuals who offer guidance, support, and encouragement aimed at developing [youth's] competence and character" (MENTOR, 2013). It is important to note that in youth mentoring, the mentor is frequently a trusted adult rather than a peer. Despite this distinction, youth mentoring continues to be relevant to peer mentoring research based in part on DuBois, Portillo, Rhodes, Silverthorn, and Valentine's (2011) meta-analysis of youth mentoring programs. This study did not find any statistical differences between program practices or outcomes when mentors were teenage peers rather than adults. This led scholars in the peer mentoring field to conclude (Karcher, 2013) that many of the best practices identified for youth mentoring (DuBois, Neville, Parra, & Pugh-Lilly, 2002) apply to peer mentoring as well, an important conclusion given that exponentially more research has been conducted on the general youth mentoring field. As stated earlier, mentorship matters, and the importance of cross-age peer mentoring appeared to be one of the more vital parts of the VIP Scholars experience.

Four

The Ripple Effect

The Influence of Mentoring on Mentors

Tyrone C. Howard, Irene Atkins, and Jon Carroll

Mentoring is the foundation upon which the VIPS program stands. From the initial moment that applicants interact with the program, relationships are formed and connections are made whereby students have the opportunity to gain access to the intellectual, social, and cultural capital of those who have already traveled a path that they are just embarking on. In the previous chapter, the authors highlighted the impact of mentoring on students in the program. The effects of that mentoring have gone far and wide as many of the program's participants have graduated in a timely fashion and subsequently pursued careers in education, medicine, law, technology, business, film, and psychology, among other fields. The students have remarked that their experiences in the VIP Scholars program, and in particular the mentoring they received, were vital ingredients in their academic success and professional pursuits. However, an unexpected outcome of the program is the influence of mentoring on the mentors. Throughout the program, we recognized the manner in which the program mentors talked consistently about how their academic interests and career paths were reaffirmed, slightly altered, significantly changed, or completely reconsidered after they served as mentors for the students. The mentors spoke at length about how the program provided time and space for them to interrogate their own identities through their relationships with the VIPS staff and students. Many of the mentors also discussed how much they grew professionally and personally after "giving back" through the various mentor–mentee relationships.

This chapter will address the multiple levels of mentoring and the influence of mentoring on mentors. All the mentors in the program were UCLA undergraduate and graduate students. The topic of mentoring's effects on mentors is important because the voices and perspectives of mentors speak to the manner in which a ripple effect or extended benefit seemed to occur throughout the program, wherein the program's aims and goals assisted not only high school students but also undergraduate and graduate students. The literature on the benefits of mentoring for youth is extensive (Ogbu & Wilson, 1990; Yancey, Siegel, & McDaniel, 2002). Youth with consistent access to mentoring do better academically and socially, are less likely to become involved in criminal activities, and are less likely to have social and emotional challenges (Bruce & Bridgeland, 2014). However, less evident in the mentoring literature are the effects of mentoring on those who serve as mentors. The role of mentoring in the VIPS program is a multifaceted one that enables mentors and mentees to engage in a nuanced relationship with the goal of moving students from high school into college while also enabling them to recognize and act upon inequality that they witness in their schools, their communities, and the wider society. We also discovered that the mentors in the VIPS program embodied an approach to mentoring that was connected to facets of critical race theory, critical pedagogy, social justice education, and other relevant educational theories to inspire students to expect excellence in the classroom and in their communities.

The mentors were instrumental in helping students to realize their own leadership potential, but they also felt inspired to do better in their own pursuits as models for their mentees. As the high school students become more involved in the VIPS program, they are encouraged to develop VIPS clubs at their schools so that students who are not directly affiliated with the program can have the opportunity to benefit from its philosophies and resources. Throughout, mentors noted that their hearing that students were taking on more active leadership roles in their high schools made mentors feel obligated to do the same at the university level. Many commented that they had assumed greater leadership roles on their college campus after discovering how much the high school students had done and that they also felt compelled to "lead by example." To facilitate this tremendous growth in students, the VIPS program employs both school year and summer program mentors. This chapter will detail the ways that mentoring is conceived of and practiced by mentors as they develop meaningful relationships with students over time. We will differentiate between the ways that mentors became involved in the program and the meaning they made of their experiences once they were in it. You will hear the voices of mentors in both depth and breadth. We will start by introducing the theoretical frames that appeared to shape the approaches of many of the mentors in the program. In this regard, issues around social justice and racial equity were quite prevalent. We will then provide a range of the voices and perspectives of the mentors from the program. These voices will speak to the value of mentoring for these mentors, how they were influenced by it, and what it means for them long term. Finally, we will go more in depth with two of the mentors as they discuss their personal journey to mentoring. Throughout the chapter, the mentors will discuss why they chose to mentor, their specific mentorship approaches, and the influences that working with students in the VIP Scholars program had on them professionally and personally. We choose to focus on the importance of mentoring because there is a critical need to assess how educational pipelines for students of color can be strengthened at all levels, including the undergraduate and graduate levels. In addition, the chapter will discuss the concept of critical race mentoring, where issues tied to race, gender, and class are explicitly at the center of how mentors choose to mentor given their multiple identities and how they play out in providing support for students of color.

MENTORSHIP MATTERS

There is evidence that mentoring programs that focus on developing positive racial identities help foster increased academic engagement and achievement (Cohen, Steele, & Ross, 1999; Ogbu & Wilson, 1990). The VIPS program takes a unique approach to mentoring relationships, which we will discuss in this chapter. Students are guided to not only survive the high school road to college in the classroom, but also identify and acquire the tools necessary to resist and deconstruct institutional oppression outside the classroom. To this end, issues tied to power, race, gender, and class are frequent topics of discussion in the program. So for many of the mentors, this critical approach to mentoring was intrinsic in their work in the program. In many ways, these approaches to mentoring are tied to the writings of Paulo Freire (1993) and the work around critical pedagogy, where issues such as oppression, struggle, and dehumanization are staples in developing critical literacies. Critical pedagogues help students identify policies, practices, and decisionmakers that prevent them and their peers from achieving academic excellence. As Andrade and Morrell (2008) note:

> Even with our obvious need to promote student voice and student empowerment, critical educators of urban adolescents cannot abdicate our responsibility to nurture, to guide, to support, to cajole, to correct, and to demand from students what they may have been socialized not to demand from themselves. (p. 102)

Andrade and Morrell (2008) also note that students should emerge from educational encounters possessing enhanced power. This is certainly part of the philosophy held by VIPS mentors as they approach their work with students. Given the significant challenge that faces mentors as they embark on their journey with students, it is worth examining their motivations for joining the VIPS program in the first place.

Mentoring relationships in VIPS are built upon recognition by both students and mentors of the influence of race in issues of equity and access in higher education and their coming to understand this influence. To that end, an explicit topic in mentors' work with the high school students was race and justice. Throughout this chapter, we use critical race theory to help us understand how the mentors engaged in their own approaches to mentoring and the influence it had on them personally and professionally. CRT enabled all the parties to understand the unique path that was being traveled and the destination to be reached.

CRITICAL RACE THEORY

Critical race theory (CRT) is used in this chapter to situate mentoring because of the manner in which race consistently emerged in conversations with mentors past and present. The application of this framework discloses the structural nature of racism and will be used to examine how racist systems continue to operate to marginalize people of color. CRT emerged out of critical legal studies (CLS) as a framework that centers race in the examination of legal systems (Bell, 1995; Crenshaw, Gotanda, Peller, & Thomas, 2000; Lynn & Parker, 2006). This viewpoint challenges the dominant ideology of race neutrality, objectivity, color blindness, and meritocracy and asserts that race has contributed to all manifestations of group advantage and disadvantage. Yosso (2005) identifies five tenets of CRT as follows:

> 1. *Intercentricity of Race and Racism*, which states that race and racism is endemic and permanent in the United States [and] a discussion on race within CRT begins with an examination of how race has been socially constructed in U.S. history and how the system of racism functions to oppress People of Color while privileging whites. A CRT analysis in education centralizes race and racism, while also focusing on racism's intersections with other forms of subordination, based on gender, class, sexuality, language, culture, immigration status, phenotype, accent, and surname.
> 2. *Challenge to Dominant Ideology*, which suggests traditional claims of race neutrality and objectivity act as a camouflage for privileged and self-interest power of dominant groups in U.S. society. A CRT framework in education challenges claims that the educational system offers objectivity, meritocracy, color blindness, race neutrality, and equal opportunity.

3. *Commitment to Social Justice* that is dedicated to advancing a social justice agenda in schools and society. Acknowledging schools as political places and teaching as a political act, CRT views education as a tool for eliminating all forms of subordination and empowering oppressed groups to transform society.

4. *Centrality of Experiential Knowledge*, whereby CRT sees the experiential knowledge of people of color as authentic, valid, and essential to understanding, analyzing, and teaching about racial subordination. Critical race research in education views this knowledge as a strength and draws explicitly on lived experiences.

5. *Interdisciplinary Perspective*, whereby CRT analyzes racism, classism, sexism, and homophobia from a historical and interdisciplinary perspective. CRT goes beyond disciplinary boundaries drawing on multiple methods to listen to and learn from those otherwise silenced by popular discourse and academic research. This tenet is used in analyzing how curriculum on history, language, culture, sexuality, homophobia, and gender affects students.

An additional aspect of CRT is the idea of "differential racialization" (Delgado & Stefancic, 2001) and what that means for people of color. The concept of differential racialization and its many consequences are important here for mentoring. Critical writers in law, as well as social science, have drawn attention to how the dominant society racializes different minority groups at different times, in response to shifting needs such as those of the labor market.

Delgado and Stefancic (2001) contend:

Closely related to differential racialization—the idea that each race has its own origins and ever evolving history—is the notion of intersectionality and anti-essentialism. No person has a single, easily stated, unitary identity. (p. 1)

The idea of different racialization is critical where mentoring is concerned, because much of the literature on mentoring defines it in a very nonracialized context. Moreover, an assumption often made about mentoring in racialized categories is that there is an overwhelming number of similarities within groups. In other words, what works for one African American student will probably work for another, or an approach to engaging one Latina student will lead to success with another. What the mentors in the VIPS program talked about as critical was the individualized approach to getting to know students, building rapport, establishing trust, and then imparting information. Given the students who are part of VIP Scholars, the schools they attend, and the colleges they pursue for postsecondary options, issues of race were typically prominent, and as the students and mentors mentioned throughout their time in the program, race matters (Howard, 2010). Mentors in the VIPS program talked about how they have been able to take their unique lived experiences as racialized students and offer advice to students about how to avoid pitfalls. For example, mentors understood the value of taking Advanced Placement (AP) or college-level coursework because of its academic capital in the college application process. They also could relate to the students' experience of often being the only Black student in AP courses. Many of the mentors could relate to the challenges of pursuing college when no one else in their immediate families had done so and the difficulty of obtaining reliable information and resources. Moreover, the mentors were able to address how issues of racism or perceived racism could be navigated and not serve as a debilitating step on the journey to college. Sam, a VIPS academic-year mentor, who supported students throughout the year, commented on this point by stating that his goal with mentoring included up-front discussions about race in his dialogues with his mentees. He tried

> to empower them like the social justice approach of basically making them more aware of who they are as Black students and their responsibility as Black students and the role as Black students like basically like any ideas of what a Black student should be and then rise to that expectation of what they would be like . . . and really empower them and make them more self-aware of their own identity.

Isis, a 1st-year mentor, stated that mentoring was quite life changing and that it needed to be race conscious. She contended:

> It [mentoring] definitely impacted me just because it's stuff that we theorize in class that you talk about superficially in class but it is real when you talk about race. So you talk to them about how to really handle these kind of situations . . . really like actually all right here is what you learn now about how to use this intervention technique as best as possible to circumvent what is going on, and . . . to help them out as much as possible when racism happens.

Jonathan, a 3rd-year undergraduate, talked about how for him mentoring was part of a larger commitment to social justice. His response to what mentoring meant to him seemed to align with CRT's social justice component, whereby schools are seen as political spaces, and the importance of providing students the skills and knowledge to navigate such spaces. He noted:

> It [mentoring] is a reaffirming fact like a reassurance to me. I was just fortunate enough to become a mentor. . . . I was like "you need to know

more about social justice issues," like having advocacy for myself or being more aware of the issues and conscious about things going on in my community. . . . I think just being part of the program it is more educational to the students about educational issues going on within high school students and how to adjust these issues.

The preceding quote suggests that the benefits of mentoring are twofold. The mentors' ability to reflect on their own practices sharpened their approach in ways that would ultimately have a positive influence on mentees. The mentors saw their roles as having two components: offering information on explicit steps in navigating complex institutions (e.g., universities), but also providing guidance on how to increase mentees' awareness of social justice concepts. The idea of social justice in mentoring was also tied to the importance of helping the students speak about their own experiences, share their stories, and affirm their realities.

Jonathan's quote above makes reference to the manner in which explicit steps and strategies were offered to many of the mentees about how to navigate intimidating and often complex institutions. Mentees continually referred to the importance of mentors' helping to demystify the college experience. The mentors stated that much of this approach was tied to building a level of comfort and trust with the students that would allow them to open up and speak about their truths. Trevor said it was important to

get to know them [students]. Getting to know their faces and like their background, where they come from, their families. Whatever they feel comfortable sharing with you on that day, you just try to get as much as you can get out of them. So just getting to know them will allow them to trust you. Then they tell you a lot about their lives, and you learn about what they are really going through.

Trevor's point about getting to know a student is important and a big part of the mentoring process. It should be noted that for many of the mentors sharing the same ethnic or racial background was viewed as a big plus for gaining the trust of the mentees. Much has been written about the salience of same-race backgrounds in mentoring. While the research is mixed about the effects of same-race mentoring (Cohen et al., 1999; Yancey et al., 2002) the mentors in VIPS talked about the potential benefits of it:

I think a lot of mentoring had to do with personal relationships with students and just a lot of us coming from the same background, being [of] either African American or Latino descent. So just being close to age,

I think with the students, and having . . . like being able to tell them the difference between what I experienced in high school and not knowing, like not being aware of what I experienced . . . like discrimination or microaggressions in classes like being the only Black student in an AP class, but then having the background knowledge of the training to deal with those things, because you can relate.

Other mentors discussed the benefits of being from similar racial and ethnic backgrounds and similar neighborhoods and schools and about closeness in age being instrumental in being able to identify with some of the challenges that students encountered:

Like being conscious and socially aware of things and being able to explain that to them while they're still in high school I think makes them more aware. 'Cause you're able to take your own experiences, which are similar to theirs, and let them know like "this is what that is." Am I making sense? . . . And to let them know "okay, yeah, I experienced this and you can get through it too."

Justine, who was only a few years removed from being a student in the program herself, discussed her desire to help the students understand the dynamics of teacher–student interactions and how race can play a role in such situations:

One thing that I wanna make sure that I do is helping them understand the dynamics of teacher and student. . . . I wound up talking to my students a lot about how they interact with teachers because of certain situations, because of like temperaments, with them being little Black boys and girls with teachers who are not Black, they don't always understand you. So just be careful.

The mentors also understood the nature of being seen as less capable by high school teachers and counselors because of their race or ethnicity at schools that have historically not sent many students to prestigious colleges and universities. Therefore, by many of the mentors' accounts they were able to explain to mentees why it is important as students of color to seek out these opportunities instead of being content with just getting good grades and only applying to local state universities. Thus, as mentors accumulated more social and academic capital throughout their journey, they felt it was a responsibility to pass on that information, through their interactions with their mentees, and to discuss how they were able to renegotiate the relationship between race and power that CRT activists are interested in transforming.

But what do these interactions mean for the mentors themselves? How did they make meaning of sharing these experiences with their students? Many mentors talked about how for them mentoring is the ultimate act of selflessness, wherein they have to put the needs of others before themselves. Kayla talked about this:

> I mean, I don't have kids, but mentoring is a huge responsibility, and being in the summer program made me realize that it is not about me. It is about helping the students.

Jackson, another summer mentor, affirmed Kayla's sentiment when he stated:

> Mentoring has stretched me so much. It made me stop being so concerned about myself and to recognize the importance of helping others. I used to think about my needs, and my wants, but mentoring forces you to put others' needs ahead of you. That was good for me to do, because it helped me grow.

The idea of giving back, being selfless, and constantly being mindful of others came across from a number of the mentors. Also prominent in the mentors' responses was that a key tenet of social justice is being willing to put others before oneself and being totally committed to someone else's personal and professional needs. London, a senior who was serving as a mentor for the 2nd year, stated:

> For me, mentoring is to make students more aware of things that are going on and why it's important that we give back to our community. So then when I came here, I felt a sense of responsibility not only to myself, but to my community, and to my students to wanna give back. And I've been involved with VIPS program ever since. I think, yeah, I think mentorship is the number one factor to consider when talking about giving back.

A core value that is imparted to the mentors in their training is the utility of group accountability. In other words, the needs of the greater good come before a person's individual needs. The mentors often seem to internalize this idea—being centered on selflessness is a way to build and maintain a sense of community. As one mentor stated, "Hopefully when they [mentees] see me putting their needs before my own, then we have trust and a better community."

IMPROVING COMMUNITY

The mentors talked about how discussing issues around race was an integral part of what they did with their mentees. Yet another theme that emerged was mentors' efforts to communicate with students about the importance of attaining an education as a way to transform and improve their communities. Giving back became a concept that they embodied in their mentoring approach and that also evolved into an explicit focus of their mentorship. Jasmyne talked about the importance of making sure that students are informed about challenges in their community and how to be agents of change:

> I think as a mentor, your number one role is just to make sure the students are informed. Informed about college, informed about their schools, and informed about changing where you come from. But your number one goal is to make sure they're informed.

Imani entered into the role of program mentor with a deep familiarity of the program, having been in it as a student several years prior. She knew firsthand the positive impact that a multidimensional mentor relationship could have on a student's academic trajectory. Given the positive role of her participation in her matriculation to UCLA, she felt inclined to "reach back" and engage in similar mentoring relationships with high school students on the same road that she traveled. When Imani arrived at UCLA, she had an immediate sense of community with fellow graduates of the VIPS program as well with as the staff who had worked with her since 10th grade. It is no wonder that she continued to work within the program as a mentor. She came into the role of mentor already equipped with many of the skills to help students navigate the high school pipeline to college. She said talking and planning with other mentors was critical in her development to support students. She stated:

> It give us [mentors] a chance to keep their perspective fresh on the ways that today's youth operate. Whether it is the way that they talk, dress, sing, dance, or utilize technology, there is capital in youth culture that we [mentors] can use to our advantage in any profession that we enter into.

FROM LEARNING TO LEADING

For mentors, mentoring led to awakening, self-reflection, and a further commitment to the goals of the VIP Scholars program. A number of the mentors talked about how their career goals were confirmed through their mentoring roles in VIP Scholars. Marlon contended that "being a mentor just reinforced my desire to work with young Black men." Another mentor asserted that the reason she is a psychology major is to help others deal with problems and the thinking behind solving complicated life challenges. She stated that being a mentor "made it even clearer in my mind that this is what I want to do." A returning mentor remarked that she was on the fence about a career in servicing youth but becoming a mentor "helped me to see the real need that we have in our communities to help others. That's the work I want to do." Thus, mentorship provides some individuals with a sense of clarity, purpose, and mission in defining the work they want to pursue professionally. For Bree, being a mentor was a huge factor in her decision to enter education:

> I always thought I wanted to go into education, but serving as a mentor, and working with the students, made it even more clear in my mind that this is what I want to do. You can see how you can really influence the future by working with students, and that is important.

For all that the mentors are able to take away from the program, there is a cost for all the time that they invest in being a VIPS mentor. This is a particular issue for mentors who are not necessarily interested in a future in education. Several of the mentors not looking to go into an education career must therefore be more strategic in accumulating experience in their field while at the same time continuing their work in the VIPS program. Another downside for the mentors is that as much as one may love doing the job, it does eventually come to an end, and for students this can mean having to start from scratch with a new mentor at an inopportune moment in the journey. Justyn, for example, ultimately had to stop mentoring as he got deeper into graduate school and needed to focus on his dissertation research. Imani stated that ultimately she graduated from UCLA and needed to pursue other professional opportunities.

Each time there is turnover of mentors at a given site, there is a chance that the pipeline of students applying to the program will suffer, depending on how well the new mentor is able to build upon what the previous mentor established at the site. Ultimately, according to the mentors, the advantages of participating in the VIPS program as a mentor far outweigh the challenges and offer a fulfilling experience for those who take on the responsibility.

For many of the mentors, the impact of being a VIPS mentor on their college experience was immeasurable and spans far and wide. Several stated that one of the more apparent outcomes of working as a mentor is improving mentors' academic mindset. As mentors educated students and trained them to develop effective study habits and skills, simultaneously, the skills that they helped the students develop were translated into their own academic life. Trenton explained:

> You can't tell your students to use their time wisely, study diligently, and then you're not doing the same thing with your studies. So it kinda forces you to practice what you preach when it comes to you studying.

For many of the mentors tips like studying material in increments, setting aside a weekly or daily study time for certain classes, meeting other classmates and forming study groups were practical skills that they shared, and they mentioned that it helped their own educational career. Other mentors stressed additional skills such as time management, prioritization, organization, planning, and following up as being central to what they taught their students, and they described how these skills soon were applied to their own lives. The mentors also realized how much the students saw them as role models. Janae explained:

> They are always watching and listening to us, so I have to be mindful of what I am doing, what I say, even what I am wearing, because they are taking note of what we say and do. I feel like you just have to always be aware of how you are influencing them on what it means to be a college student. I never thought that would be a big part of this work.

The mentors also discussed how soon certain skills and practices were applied to their own lives—in a way, besides mentors becoming big brothers or big sisters to their mentees, by holding the students accountable to rising to their academic potential, many mentors almost played a mentoring role for other mentors, as they held themselves accountable to improving as college students, asked about other mentors' courses, and offered another layer of accountability. Destiny mentioned:

> One of the things that I got out of mentoring that I never expected to get was the way the other mentors supported each other. Some of us were taking classes while we were mentoring so it helped having people support you.

According to many of the mentors, the workplace norm centered on improving, perfecting, and challenging oneself academically, because these same things are what they all sought to instill in their students. Of course, not all mentors' academic lives have been positively influenced by the leadership role of being a mentor, but the mentors were unanimous in asserting that the best way to effectively motivate another person to excel academically is to lead by example. Destiny stated, "One of the most profound effects being a mentor has had on me is that it has given me the unique opportunity to be a part of a familial community with my fellow mentors. We make up a network of support for each other." The importance of community for the mentors is vital and having a feeling of a sustained and integrated network of support is crucial for the academic persistence of underrepresented students of color at predominantly White institutions. Astin (1975, 1987, 1993) emphasizes the significance of involvement in the learning and development process of any individual. Essentially, his theory holds that the more a student is involved and connected to a community of learners, the more likely it is that the student will be integrated in the undergraduate academic and social experience. Tinto's (1975, 1987, 1993) theory posits that a higher degree of involvement leads to persistence and academic success, something that was mentioned by several of the mentors in VIPS. Several referred to how they actually studied more while they were mentoring or how they were on the same time schedule as students, and that forced them to be more disciplined in their study habits and courses.

In the VIPS office, the mentors frequently joined together for general dialogue about life, school, their work as mentors, and how they could best master what they do in order to have the influence on mentees that other mentors had on them. Through these daily discussions, mentors learned more about the personal lives of their coworkers and also more about themselves. The VIPS office became a space where they informed one another about resources, events on campus, and which classes to take and avoid. In this dedicated weekly meeting they brought up philosophical, cultural, or political issues they had been wrestling with on campus. The mentors stated that they even had critical, but friendly, debates, which deepened their understanding of social justice issues. The VIPS office was also where they vented about their most pressing obstacles or personal battles. In this 200-square-foot office, mentors received encouragement and guidance to help them in the professional work they did for the students; further, many stated that it was where they grew and developed as scholars and as individuals.

"PRACTICING WHAT WE PREACH"

A less noticeable impact of working as an academic year mentor comes in the beginning of the academic year, when mentors are faced with the task of recruiting 10th-graders to the program. The most significant aspect of the recruitment process is the mentors' approach to explaining the program to students. The majority of the academic year mentors are previous high school participants in the program themselves, so many of the mentors stated that they relied on their own personal experience to offer students a compelling reason to apply to the program. Mentors subconsciously engage in deep self-reflection about the impact the program has had on their lives. Over half the mentors stated that mentoring gave them a better understanding of their own educational trajectories and how they have come to be at UCLA after having just been in those 10th-graders' shoes. Austin said:

> You realize how time goes by fast, because we were just where they are, and how our time as undergraduates will go fast. So just as they are preparing for college, we are also thinking and preparing for graduate school. . . . So I stress to [high school] students, this is your future.

One of the more consistent themes raised by the mentors was that mentoring pushed them to think more astutely about their own educational goals and objectives beyond their time as undergraduates, or as one mentor described it, "practicing what we preach." The ongoing conversations about the importance of strong grades, studying, preparing, engaging in time management, doing well on high-stakes tests such as the ACT and SAT, and developing a well-rounded set of experiences resulted in many of the mentors asking themselves if they were doing the same thing for their graduate school prospects. The mentors consistently stated that they never realized how much mentoring would help them think deeply about their own educational priorities and goals. Will told us during one interview:

> So when the students asked me "what was I doing after I graduated?" I had to think about it. . . . I didn't want to say "I don't know," so I started doing my own research on grad school programs so that I could tell them what I was planning to do next after UCLA.

Other mentors talked about how as students talked about SAT prep, they began thinking about GRE or LSAT prep. A number of mentors also discussed that they mentioned university application deadlines to mentees; this forced mentors to think about their own deadlines for law school, medical school, or other graduate programs. In short, the idea of assisting students in preparation for the next phase of their academic careers sharpened the thinking and preparation for the mentors in a way that most said they never expected. The benefits of these tasks for mentors should not be overlooked. A significant body of work looks at the effects of stereotype threat on college students of color and women undergraduates (Steele, 1997, 1998; Steele & Aronson, 1995). According to scholars of stereotype threat, one way to reduce or eliminate the effects of stereotype threat is to allow people to affirm their self-worth. That is, demonstrating or discussing a task or skill in which one has a high degree of proficiency not only has the potential to help others but also can consciously or subconsciously assist the person with reducing his or her own internalization of the stereotype. Researchers state that this affirmation of self-worth can be achieved by encouraging people to think about the gifts, characteristics, skills, values, or roles that they possess and value or view as important (Frantz, Cuddy, Burnett, Ray, & Hart, 2004; Schimel, Arndt, Banko, & Cook, 2004). This self-worth can be encouraged through demonstrating how individuals have had success, articulating to others ways that they can attain success, or expressing consistently what needs to be done, and how, to accomplish challenging tasks. The concept of self-worth is important here because for many mentors, the constant references to what is required to get into college and to be successful there increased their own sense of efficacy and self-worth.

The mentors consistently stated that they understand that their mentors at VIPS aided them in the college attainment and success journey, in getting to where they are now, and many felt that they would not have made it to UCLA if not for the program. This impelled them to express this clearly to the 10th-graders, and repeatedly, since they have to make countless presentations to multiple groups of eligible students. The mentors' reflections of VIPS and the importance of the mentorship appeared to go deeper with every presentation.

REFLECTING ON MENTORSHIP

In the following we present two firsthand accounts from mentors in the program. One (Irene Atkins) served in the program as a student and then went on to become a mentor in the program; the other (Jon Carroll), a graduate student, served as an academic year mentor.

Irene Atkins

Personally, I would always talk about the importance of mentoring in my presentation to students; I would discuss how vividly I remember my mentor Neshamah calling me out of class to talk to me about the program. I reflect on how much my life has been positively affected just because Neshamah called me down to discuss the VIPS program. Through this process, I began to see myself as having the potential to affect other students' lives just as Neshamah had affected mine. Put simply, the experience of recruiting gave me purpose and helped me recognize the power of the work I was doing. From those moments onward, I knew I wanted to spend my lifetime changing the life trajectories of hundreds of students.

I was a freshman when I had the opportunity to become a VIPS mentor. And because the majority of my coworkers were 2 or 3 years ahead of me in school, they provided me with invaluable navigational capital, giving me inside knowledge on how to be a successful UCLA student. Picking up on their conversations gave me a huge advantage in getting ahead in my undergraduate career. Educational scholar Tara Yosso (2005) defines "navigational capital" as

> skills of maneuvering through social institutions. Historically, this infers the ability to maneuver through institutions not created with Communities of Color in mind. For example, strategies to navigate through racially-hostile university campuses draw on the concept of academic invulnerability, or students' ability to "sustain high levels of achievement, despite the presence of stressful events and conditions that place them at risk of doing poorly at school and, ultimately, dropping out of school." (p. 80)

The incorporation of navigational capital is precisely what VIPS mentors pass down and consistently share with one another. Inclusion in this community of resources gives mentors the navigational capital to not only get through undergraduate school but also succeed in the graduate and professional school arena.

As a low-income, first-generation student of color, I did not even conceive of attaining an advanced degree. Attending UCLA as an undergraduate seemed like a major feat and, therefore, the end of the road for my educational career. It was not until I found myself surrounded by a multitude of individuals matriculating through the educational pipeline who came from backgrounds similar to mine, did I began to realize I too had the potential to advance my education. It was also the constant stream of positive affirmations I received from them about my ability that gave me the confidence to continue with my higher education. Not only was I finally able to conceive of obtaining a master's or doctoral degree; I was also acknowledging that in my career, I could be more than just a worker in the education system. I could restructure, contribute to, and innovate the education system by running programs, changing policies, and heading up my own nonprofit organization or consulting. Being a mentor really helped me to develop this sense of myself that I did not know could be possible.

Through working for VIP Scholars, I also had the privilege of gaining meaningful professional development that would give me the foundational tools to ultimately branch out and make waves in the education field. VIPS mentors go through a series of counseling training at the beginning of every school year and continue in professional development through weekly meetings. But even beyond the intended development activities, mentors have the unique experience of developing skills from on-the-job duties. Mentors gain skills from having to network with parents and guardians and build networks and professional relationships with school administration, staff, faculty, counselors, and sometimes even school board members.

The Impact of Being a Summer Mentor. The role of the mentors is invaluable in the VIPS program. In many ways, the mentors serve as a buffer between the students and program staff. The mentors live on campus during the summer program and get to know the students perhaps better than anyone else. Time is structured so that these mentors are with the students around the clock as counselors and confidantes and have the opportunity to develop a deeper connection with students and know them more holistically than do academic year mentors, who are primarily focused on developing a student's coursework and academic identity. As summer mentors we have an increased opportunity to help develop a student's academic skill set because of opportunities to spend time tutoring one on one, while academic year mentors have to be more resourceful in addressing a student's academic needs.

Being a summer mentor has its own impact and unique lessons that could not be acquired during the academic year. Not only does being a summer mentor deepen one's sense of responsibility for the safety and well-being of others, but it also opens up one's mind about the range of experiences and diversity any group of people can bring to a space. Because summer mentors are living with the students and engulfed in their affairs all day, every day, we learn so much from the students' lives. For me personally, being a summer mentor made me realize what it takes to affect a student's life. I learned that I have to be a good listener and that being an effective mentor does not mean telling students what to do; it means facilitating their development in such a way that allows them to find the answers for themselves. After being a summer mentor I became less judgmental. As human beings, we all naturally judge, but it is important to have experiences that teach us to open our minds to the complexity of other human beings. I unconsciously minimized my natural tendency to judge after getting to know so many individuals on a deep, personal level (both colleagues and students). They definitely did not live up to my preconceived notions about who they were, and I began to see them as whole students, not just who they appeared to be on paper.

Being a summer mentor also challenged me to open up and explore myself further. Mentors have to set an example for honesty, openness, and vulnerability, so I also had to come to terms with what I was dealing with to effectively guide my students. They truly were interested in my life stories and about how I overcame my obstacles. There is such value in storytelling, and so many meaningful lessons learned on both sides of the experience. The precise impact summer mentoring has had on me may look different for my coworkers. However, I can say with certainty that the one impact it had on us all is the unquestionable strength and passion we developed. Both the strength and passion gave us purpose in life, and I have no doubt that we will continue to carry these life lessons with us as we create a meaningful life journey for ourselves and those around us.

My Introduction to Mentoring: Jon Carroll

At the time I mentored in the program, I was a 3rd-year PhD student. I believed that taking the time to mentor students provided a perfect way to remain connected to youth as I worked toward completing my doctoral studies. For me, mentoring meant providing a pathway for opportunities that I was afforded as a high school student or a "link to college." I approached mentoring in a very serious and thoughtful way. I believed that people had invested in me, so it was only fitting that I try to invest in others in a similar way. I would not have gotten involved in the VIPS program had I not met and gotten to know the program director. Both the director and I were graduate students at the time we met, and we had the same urban education concentration. During the 2008 American Educational Research Association conference, we discussed the director's work with the VIPS program. I was intrigued by the idea of a program that was designed specifically to bring students of color to UCLA, a campus that I found to be less diverse than the University of Pennsylvania campus, where I spent my undergraduate years. I was eager to participate in any initiative that would satisfy my desire to "give back" and use my accumulated knowledge as a student to help others. I would say that in many ways mentoring only affirmed my desire to work with young people. It is one of the most important ways to give back.

I came to graduate school intending to focus my research on the examination of identity. I wanted to better understand how the attitudes that students hold most dear about themselves affect the ways that they approach education and ultimately fare academically. For example, if being Black is central to your identity, how does the way you define Blackness inform your attitude toward school? These questions are particularly intriguing as they pertain to African American males because of the existing and growing body of work that indicates how poorly African American male students are doing in school as compared with their peers of other ethnicities on many achievement markers. The VIPS program provided a number of opportunities to explore the answers to these questions from a number of different perspectives because of the variety of schools where the program is situated.

Mentoring provided me with a sense of what it means to work with high school students, but beyond this, one of its immediate benefits is that it provides mentors with a firsthand look at the inner workings of Los Angeles–area schools. It is one thing to theoretically understand what happens on urban campuses, but it is different to see things unfold live and in front of you, seeing the challenges that students face with teachers, counselors, and administrators. For example, I saw firsthand how disheartening it is to know that students of color face disparate rates of suspension, yet it is more alarming to witness a student fight and see how teachers, administrators, and law enforcement move to criminalize students in ways that prevent students from being able to participate in the classroom. I would not have gotten this experience without being in schools, working with my mentees, and just observing school culture and school practices. In many ways, the practices explain why more students do not get to college.

One of the most important things I learned about mentoring is the value of relationships. Forming relationships is so important to connecting with students. Some might ask, "How do you form relationships with students?" I would say that it is about listening, and not judging. It is also about confiding in students your own challenges in schools and life so that they can see you as a human being just like them. I would also say that it is critical to understand as much as possible about students' academic experiences and even learning about their lives outside schools can also be helpful in building relationships with students of color.

Finally, I would say that it is important to engage in conversations with the students on a wide range of topics and events. So I would talk to the students about many different issues, such as interracial dating; we would talk about media representation of people of color; we would talk about all these different things, as mentors and as people who have taken on these classes and experiences. We would also discuss hegemony and how it plays out in schools. We know what institutionalized racism is and for them they are kind of coming into it, so just like asking, okay, well who came up with that? You know. We would discuss "Who says this is the standard? Where do we see that? Okay, that's the media. Who owns the media? Do we own it? Okay, what would happen if we owned it?" Just like different things that, to kind of problematize it for them and also encourage them to ask these questions and instead of just being given answers.

CONCLUSION

Jon and Irene offer different viewpoints on how to think about mentoring. In Irene's case, being a student in the program gave her a way to give to others the same types of things that were given to her when she was a high school student. The sense of giving back was clear. Irene also talked about peer mentoring, which enhanced her experience through talking with other mentors, many of whom were older but still had useful information. While many mentoring models tend to be vertical in scope, Irene's case sheds light on the utility of horizontal mentoring, which is rarely examined yet can be equally beneficial. Finally, Irene talked about the manner in which mentoring led her to engage in self-examination, or reflecting on her processes in serving youth. Her comments suggested a sentiment about continually asking herself what she knew, what she heard, and how she could get better at mentoring. Needless to say, self-examination has a number of benefits for those in the practitioner world, and Irene outlines tangible ways of how that process aided her mentoring practices.

Jon's account gives insight into how mentoring can inform researchers. As someone who was interested in examining research on identity at the time, mentoring allowed him to put theory into practice, by observing how high school youth made sense of the college-going process. Jon's account seemed to also make clear how race matters. He cultivated relationships with high school students by not being afraid to engage in racial dialogues; his insight into this process is important for those wanting to cultivate meaningful mentoring relationships with youth. Jon also highlights the complexity that is involved in navigating high school. Seeing firsthand some of the challenges that students had with teachers and counselors engendered empathy and helped him think about how he could better serve his students, because he saw the limitations and could precisely align his support in the areas where he knew the schools fell short.

It goes without saying that mentorship is one of the more selfless acts one can engage in. In many ways, mentorship in all its manifestations is the cornerstone of the VIPS program. The idea is inherent in many practices and throughout the program that low-income students of color, many of whom would be first-generation college-goers, have the potential to be successful at the college level. The reason that more are not in college is situated not in a deficit approach to their intellect but in a critique of how educational institutions have fallen short in providing them the necessary knowledge, skills, and contacts needed for college access. Here is where mentoring comes into play. Throughout the program the mentors shared the challenges, frustrations, and difficulties associated with the role of mentor. While program personnel heard these concerns, what was abundantly clear was that each and every mentor stated that if given the opportunity, he or she would do it again—hence, demonstrating the rewards of mentoring.

As universities consider ways of identifying, recruiting, supporting, and retaining low-income students of color it is critical to establish a core group of individuals, programs, and institutional policies that promote sustained mentorship. These mentoring roles can manifest in numerous ways, and we do not advocate a one-size-fits-all approach to mentorship. However, we do believe that there should be a careful approach to the key takeaways that program participants are expected to acquire and to who the individuals are who are best suited to pass on that information. Ironically, many of the students who served as mentors in the VIP Scholars program did not think they would be good mentors and had internal doubts about their ability to help others. However, what became evident over time was how many of the mentors embraced, reveled in, and ultimately became quite proficient in their mentorship roles. It was also evident at the end of each 2-week and 5-week summer program how students felt about the mentors. At every program's closing ceremonies, students are allowed to share with the audience any words, thoughts, or expressions of gratitude they wish to impart. Overwhelmingly, students had high praise for their mentors. Consistent references to the mentors included how much "they cared about us," how mentors "invested in us," and "the life-changing way" mentors connected to students. These comments speak volumes about how mentorship matters in the lives of young people.

Although the benefits to mentees are clear, what this chapter demonstrates is the way that mentoring affects mentors. Over the past 10 years, we have discovered that a number of mentors have changed majors, taken on new jobs, or redefined their career pathways because of what they learned about mentoring. This was not an expected outcome of the program. In many ways, it has been a pleasant surprise and a most intriguing finding. In short, mentoring matters. It matters because it enhances the lives of all involved. It also matters because it picks up where institutional support falls short. Finally, it matters because those who provide it often feel as profoundly changed as do the benefactors of their time, support, knowledge, and concern thought the mentoring process. While issues around gender, race, ethnicity, age, and experiences should all be considered when selecting mentors, it is abundantly clear from our data over 10 years that conviction and compassion about social justice, equity, and the belief in underserved populations and communities lie at the heart of this work. As we saw throughout the data with our mentors, while the work is demanding and can even be grueling at times, one cannot put a value on knowing that others' lives are the smallest bit improved because of what mentors have given them.

Five

Community Voices

Justyn Patterson and Ashley V. Williams

The ripple effects of the VIP Scholars program reverberate beyond the co-hort students. In the period of 10 years, the program has affected numerous family members, school administrators, and cohort peers alike. This is by design. The program was designed to support students on multiple fronts while simultaneously providing support to multiple program stakeholders. High school partners become active partners, whereby the primary point of contact, usually the college counselor, meets with VIPS program administrators throughout the academic year and interacts with the program mentors weekly. This work would not be possible without the support of university faculty and administrators. From the beginning, the vice provost's office has dedicated financial and human resources to the program, and faculty members from the Graduate School of Education have been critical partners as well. The most vital partners are the parents/guardians of the student participants, being essential to the program's success. Parents/guardians are required to become actively involved in their scholars' VIPS experience from program entry interviews to mandatory attendance at Saturday Academies. The following chapter will highlight the voices of VIPS parents and guardians. The VIPS model has always recognized the role of parents and families on the academic achievement of students. They are intentionally included as partners in the effort to provide support to VIPS students. As such, parents are able to offer a unique perspective on the VIPS experience and its impact on their children. They also provide insight into the impact of VIPS participation on them as partners and participants. Outreach and support programs across the country will see value in the insights of parents and guardians. This chapter will highlight the manner in which parents are involved in the program, the impact of the program on their children, and the lessons that they themselves have learned throughout the process.

PARENT ENGAGEMENT

Although there is no universal agreement about the type of parental participation that affects academic achievement, the data show that parental engagement leads to positive academic outcomes (Fan & Chen, 2001). For economically disadvantaged students and students of color, parental engagement becomes increasingly more important as the students navigate schooling environments that are not always designed for their success (Ingram, Wolfe, & Lieberman, 2007). There are numerous ways in which parents can be involved in their children's education. Grolnick and Slowiaczek (1994) identify three possible ways. First, parents may exhibit engagement through school-specific *behaviors* such as visiting the classroom or attending school-sponsored events like open houses or back-to-school nights or helping with homework. Second, parents may demonstrate engagement in a more *personal* manner that affects the student's affective experiences. In the personal domain, parents may influence a child's affective experiences with education by showing that they care about school through the conversations they have with their child about school or knowing what the child is struggling with in school. The third type of parent engagement, *cognitive/intellectual*, is centered on the exposure that a child has to intellectually stimulating experiences in the home, as in reading books, discussing current events, or visiting museums. The research suggests that parent engagement is related to not only an increase in academic skill for minority students (Jeynes, 2003) but also pro-achievement outcomes such as increased attendance, lower absenteeism, improved self-esteem, higher positive feelings toward school, and increased academic engagement (Hara & Burke, 1998; Jones, 2001; Quigley, 2000).

The VIPS program promotes engagement, rather than involvement, in parents/guardians. Parent involvement generally refers to parents' participation in activities that support their children. Activities such as attending parent conferences or assisting students with homework fall into the parent involvement domain. By contrast, parent engagement involves true partnership between the program and families (Reynolds, 2014). When engagement is the objective, parents have an active voice in establishing goals for their students, maintain ongoing relationships with the staff, and program offerings are created to be culturally responsive and support the best interest of individuals and the collective. VIPS administrators believe that as parents become more engaged in their sons' and daughters' education, their likelihood for academic achievement and postsecondary admission increases. Parent engagement with the VIP Scholars program begins at step one. When families apply to the program and interview for admission, parents and students are asked to describe what they envision the student gaining from the program and to articulate the student's needs as well as their educational, professional, and social goals. According to the VIPS director:

> Students come to our program with very different needs. Some are performing extremely well academically but need to further develop their leadership skills. Other students are involved in their schools and community but have academic needs. We also have students who are introverts, may feel isolated, and can benefit from being in a community environment. They are looking for a place where they fit in. By having parents and students identify their goals for program participation we are able to design an experience that meets their specific needs.

Parent engagement with prospective VIPS students goes beyond the written application process. Prior to program admission both the student and his or her parent must participate in an in-person interview with program administrators. The VIPS director asserts that involving the parents in this step is critical because "it establishes our expectation for participation and active engagement from the outset. We want parents to know that the relationship we are forging extends beyond the student, but it is a family relationship. They have a role to play too." Interview participation has another role as well. The program uses the interview process as a way to model how parents can be involved as advocates in their children's educational pursuits regardless of their socioeconomic or educational backgrounds. Numerous studies show that parents' educational attainment and socioeconomic status influence parent engagement in education (Grolnick, Benjet, Kurowski, & Apostoleris, 1997; Perna & Titus, 2005; Reynolds, 2014; Rowan-Kenyon, Bell, & Perna, 2008). Engaging the parents from the initial stages of program involvement begins to set the standard for what will be required of VIPS families as a part of program participation, and the type of behavior that VIPS parents will adopt in all facets of their children's education.

Parent engagement in VIPS extends beyond the initial interview process. The core of parent engagement is participation in Saturday Academies. These academies have a threefold purpose. Like the interviews, they are meant to encourage the participation of parents in their children's educational endeavors. Their value extends beyond facilitating participation. These Saturday programs are designed to increase parents' knowledge about college while simultaneously increasing their social capital through the relationships they forge with other parents and with program administrators. The VIPS program makes allowances for students who do not have parents who can attend the Saturday Academies. When parents or legal guardians are unable to attend, other caregivers, such as older siblings, grandparents, coaches, or other mentors, can attend in their stead. "For us," says the VIPS assistant director, "our intention is to help cultivate the community of support around our students. So it doesn't matter if a parent or another influential caregiver attends. We simply see ourselves as developing or strengthening our participants' support network."

SATURDAY ACADEMY

Parents and family members express an appreciation for Saturday Academies as a space for them to analyze social inequalities with other adults and for their children to work toward changing the conditions that contribute to structural injustice in their schools. Parents and family members relay that the Saturday Academy space is one in which they learn how to be assets and advocate for change in their students' schools and their own communities. Thus, in working together, VIPS staff, students, and their families learn and organize for social action together during Saturday Academies. The network of parents creates opportunities for building youths' social capital as parents share resources and plan collective action with adults (Ginwright & James, 2002; Jarrett, 1995).

According to the VIPS assistant director, each Saturday Academy is designed with a specific focus and goal in mind for both students and parents. The academies are held once a quarter and require attendance by all VIPS students—including those who are not summer program participants—and their parents. Rising juniors and rising seniors attend separate Saturday Academies during the fall and spring quarters to ensure that they along with their parents receive information that is pertinent to success during their academic year.

The first Saturday Academy attended by students and parents occurs in May of the students' 10th-grade year. During this initial orientation academy, the VIPS director and assistant director provide an overview of statistics pertaining to African American academic trajectories in comparison with those of other racial/ethnic groups. For many parents this is the first time they have been presented with and thought about the context of African American academic achievement. "I never really thought about how serious of an issue it is that our [African American] students are not going to college at the same rate as Latinos, Asians, and Whites. I just thought they didn't want to go or they weren't working hard enough but I can see how other things come into play," said a Cohort 1 parent.

From the inaugural academy, VIPS staff introduce parents to the idea of critical consciousness by challenging them to not only understand the overall African American student narrative but also take action to demand necessary resources from their schools. Further, VIPS Saturday Academies serve as a resource for information to parents and students that is often lacking in their schools. During the fall Saturday Academy, the high school juniors and their parents review various scenarios that simulate the types of obstacles they may encounter throughout the students' academic experience. Along with VIPS mentors, parents and students brainstorm effective troubleshooting strategies and act them out in role-playing format. As one Cohort 8 parent describes it, "Saturday Academies really allow us as working parents, who would otherwise not have the time, to really come together and share ideas and strategies that could help us advocate for our students effectively." Further, this parent states that the academies allow the parents to form a subcommunity within VIPS that works together to support each cohort of students.

During the fall Saturday Academy, parents of the senior VIPS students learn about the college application process and best ways to support their child throughout the process. For many senior VIPS students and parents, the fall Saturday Academy is their primary source of college information. "I'm grateful for VIPS because without this program I would not have known how to assist my daughter while she was applying to college," stated a Cohort 5 parent. "The college counselor at her school was inefficient but I could come [to Saturday Academy] or call her mentor and get more information about the FAFSA, application fees and all the tests she had to take." Parents understand VIPS to be an important resource that supplements what is offered at their child's school.

Both juniors and seniors attend the winter Saturday Academy along with their parents and families. Parents start the day in separate groups based on their scholar's grade level. Junior parents attend a workshop focused on supporting their child's passion. Parents of former VIPS high school students are invited to this workshop as panelists to share their insights on adapting to the students' transition into young adulthood and choosing a career path that encompasses their own unique passion. "For some parents the idea of letting their child choose their own career path that may not be what they envisioned for them is difficult," remarked a Cohort 1 parent who participates in the panel every year. She continued, "Of course we all want our kids to be successful but sometimes it can be scary to think they may want to take a more nontraditional route like not becoming a doctor or lawyer. Sometimes we don't even know alternative options so that's why I like sitting on the panel because I've supported my daughter through her own nontraditional journey even when I didn't fully understand." One of VIPS's goals is to ensure that students bring a social justice lens to whatever university they attend or career field they enter; thus it is important to cultivate their passions accordingly with programmatic and parental support.

After their separate sessions, the parents come together for a joint session, where they meet based on the school their child attends. Once in their groups, parents discuss the context of their students' school, including the school's API score[1] as well as various issues on the campus and within the surrounding community. This allows for seamless communication and collaboration between parents with students who attend the same school as well as with those whose students attend another VIPS partner school. Parents construct an action plan with proposed resolutions to the issues they have identified and present them to the entire group. As a whole, parents give one another feedback on their action plans and are exposed to an array of ideas. Participants become more aware of what is happening at the other VIPS schools, bringing new perspectives to what could happen at their student's campus. Further, parents find similarities across campuses to gain an even more in-depth understanding of the main adversities that affect students of color across the Los Angeles and Pasadena high schools.

The spring Saturday Academies are dedicated to preparing students and parents for summer and the upcoming academic school year in advance. Junior students and parents learn more about their second installment of the summer program, plan a budget for their senior year, and participate in a comprehensive workshop that gives an overview of their college options. Parents particularly appreciate the senior year budget activity, as demonstrated by one Cohort 4 parent's remark: "I needed him to see just how much college applications and visits would cost so that we know how to prioritize when it comes to prom and other extracurricular senior activities."

Senior students and parents attend a ceremony during which they are celebrated for their tenure as VIPS high school students. During this final Saturday Academy, students also announce which college/university they will attend in the fall. "This is just a really powerful moment where we get to see how all the hard work pays off. To see all these young, Black people going off to different parts of the country, to Ivy League universities and top-tier schools is just amazing," stated one Cohort 8 parent during the final academy. She continued, "Hopefully everyone keeps in touch through Facebook and stuff because we are a VIPS family. I'm so proud of everyone!" This parent's statement reflects hope that the VIPS family continues after the high school component. Further, this parent recognizes that VIPS staff, families, and students work in unison to ensure that Black students attend flagship universities where they have been historically underrepresented.

As noted, the VIPS family extends beyond participating students. In fact, friends and family members of VIPS students eventually join the program as

---

1. The API is a single number, ranging from a low of 200 to a high of 1000, which reflects a school's or student group's performance level based on statewide assessments.

well when they are eligible to apply. Parents often arrange carpools not only to transport VIPS students to Saturday Academies but also to bring neighbors and church youth members. "These kids need this information and if I can bring them when their own families can't, then I will," said one Cohort 5 parent. VIPS parents and families are as much a part of the program as the students. The Saturday Academy space helps parents cultivate the necessary skills and information to build a foundation of advocacy and social action within communities throughout Los Angeles and Pasadena.

FAMILY DAY

Another space created in the VIPS program that includes parental engagement is Family Day. Family Day is held the first weekend of the VIPS summer program. Families are invited to a potluck picnic at the university where they participate in games and fellowship in an informal setting. Family Day was instituted in 2010 after parents expressed a desire to commune outside the academically charged Saturday Academy space. "This is a good time for older VIPS families to meet the new families before the Saturday Academy in the winter, and this way we're just hanging out and bonding," said a Cohort 8 parent. Further, families get better acquainted with VIPS summer mentors and coordinators as well as hear their students present what they have been learning in the summer program.

In 2010, because of funding restraints, VIPS transitioned its 1st-year summer residential program from a 3-week format to a 2-week stay. Students remain on campus for the entire 2 weeks instead of, in the previous format, going home on weekends. For many students, this is the first time they are away from home and a 2-week duration can cause anxiety for both students and parents. Family Day helps to alleviate some of that anxiety by bringing families and students together halfway through the residential component. Students present examples of work they have completed during their first week, perform skits, and describe their experience in the summer program thus far. "Parents, I know you're wondering what we're doing with your babies every day," joked the assistant director during Family Day 2015, "so this is your chance to hear from them what we do." One Cohort 9 parent affirmed the program goals and structure during Family Day, saying, "I was nervous sending [my son] off but this is what it will be like when he goes to college and as I can see, [VIPS staff] is doing great work with him. I'm so proud and glad we could be a part of this."

Through Saturday Academies and Family Day, the VIPS program takes an active approach to engaging parents and caregivers in the support system of the VIPS students. Approximately 150 parents participated in focus groups and more than 170 responded to surveys. The following sections detail the most salient findings about parents who participated in VIPS programs.

INCREASED COLLEGE KNOWLEDGE AND GROWING CONSCIOUSNESS

One significant hindrance to parent participation in schools is their perceptions of their own self-efficacy, or their belief that they do not have the requisite knowledge or experience to assist their child (Bandura, 1997; Green, Walker, Hoover-Dempsey, & Sandler, 2007; Hoover-Dempsey & Sandler, 1997). Parents' low self-efficacy is often compounded by school environments that often do not have an inviting climate for parents to interact with teachers and counselors (Epstein & Dauber, 1991; Hoover-Dempsey & Sandler, 1997). VIPS Saturday Academy sessions are a space where parents can come learn how they can support their children without trepidation. As one parent Saturday Academy participant stated:

> I feel comfortable asking questions that I'm not quite sure if other people may have. VIPS has been that place where I can come and ask those questions just to get clarification on something I might hear other parents say or just to add to my knowledge of things I thought I understood.

Another parent, when describing her perception of the program, alluded to why parents feel comfortable with VIPS. She recognized the commitment of the staff and mentors as the reason that she felt positive about VIPS. She explained, "Everybody is speaking the same language, everybody has the same motivation . . . and heart about encouraging and supporting our youth." When parents feel comfortable with the environment where their children are, the conditions are established for them to participate fully.

VIPS Saturday Academies fill some of the gaps that may exist in the college knowledge of parent participants. One parent participant commented:

> VIPS is an informative program for students and parents. . . . It's more informative for me than my child. He knows more, so it's really helping me out more as a parent to know what I have to do and things I have to focus on to get my son, put him in the right direction to go to college.

Another parent commented on the value of "learning about the various aspects of applying to college and what the criteria is for getting into universities." The increase in knowledge for parents goes beyond learning about college requirements, the college application process, or ways to finance a college education. Parents who attended the Saturday Academies also found that their level of critical consciousness increased. The VIPS director structures the parents' sessions to expose the parents to data and research related to their children's college-going aspirations. She said, "Our students attend schools that do not historically have high college-going rates for African American students. We want the parents to understand exactly what they are up against as we work with them to propel their children to higher education." During one of the first academy sessions, parents are presented with college-going statistics disaggregated by race/ethnicity and socioeconomic status. During a focus group session, a parent said:

> One of the things that struck me with some of the stats [was] the small percentage of minorities that are . . . actually getting to college. . . . It hasn't really gotten much better. And it's starting to weigh heavy on my heart as to what sort of things that we can do as parents of color to really make that shift. . . . Because our kids are too talented and are smart. . . . [They need] a supportive environment that allows them to flourish and grow and be all they can be and I think that we have got to put our heads together and see how we can do that.

The awakening that this parent experienced is precisely what the Saturday Academies are created for, to inform and transform. An important component of this process involves parents role-playing with students and VIPS staff various scenarios on how to best advocate for their child back at their schools. VIPS administrators and university faculty stated that they do not believe that they can single-handedly alter the academic trajectories of their students. However, an informed and active parent base can make a significant impact on VIPS students' lives.

PARENT NETWORKS

Many parents of color have limited access to the social capital that aids in academic achievement (Auerbach, 2007; Bourdieu, 1986; Carter, 2008; McDonough, 2005b; Noguera, 2003). Social capital is defined as the quantity and quality of resources that one can obtain based upon one's position in the social hierarchy and is determined in part by wealth and the personal and professional networks within which one operates (Lin, 2000; McDonough, 1997; Stanton-Salazar & Dornbusch, 1995). The Saturday Academies are a mechanism through which parents have the opportunity to create or strengthen an academically charged network. During a 2012 focus group, a parent said:

VIPS parent interactions where we had a chance to exchange, I think that's an invaluable source. . . . I think it's very commendable that the VIPS team takes the time to gather resource information like this and to promote us interacting. And not only that, you promote other organizations in the community that are helpful for other students. You don't hold this in your head real tight and only promote one program; you let us know about other things that are available too. . . . You're naming a lot of different other programs that are available to the students out there. And it's good for the parents to be able to hear and network and things like that.

This parent identified the importance of sharing resources, including information about other programs, which can support their students' academic success. VIPS data suggest that many of the parents have a limited knowledge about resources available for assisting them with their sons' and daughters' college pursuits, but the parent sessions help to increase their collective knowledge. Other parents echoed this parent's feelings about the importance of working together and learning from one another. One parent mentioned that she learned to "become more comfortable with approaching teachers and . . . getting the information that she needs [about her daughter]," and she attributed her willingness to interact with teachers to another parent in the cohort. Still another parent commented:

I think [interacting with parents] is powerful, especially having the parents from prior [cohorts] share their experiences and hearing from their perspective with their kids that are already in juniors in college. . . . It's reassuring as a parent to have that community, have that support. . . . You don't feel alone.

The VIPS program creates spaces within Saturday Academy and Family Day not only for staff to talk to parents but also for parents to engage with one another to listen, share, strategize, and advise. Parent participants found their time together to be an invaluable opportunity for gaining knowledge about college and learning from one another through sharing resources and individual experiences. In effect, the VIPS academies were an opportunity for parents to increase their social capital.

PARENTS ADOPT NEW BEHAVIORS

The knowledge gained and the relationships developed are important, but the application of the newly acquired knowledge is paramount in the academic success of the VIP Scholars. After participating in several academies, parents adopted various practices to support their children's academic efforts. Consistent with Grolnick and Slowiaczek's (1994) parent engagement model, parents demonstrated multiple ways that they became involved with their children's education. Some became engaged through new pro-school behaviors. A Cohort 7 parent discussed how she had increased her communication with her child's teachers. She was unable to attend back-to-school night, so instead she set up individual meetings with the teachers to discuss her daughter. She explained, "It was wonderful because I got a chance to communicate with the teachers . . . and f[ound] out what was expected of her as a student. . . . I stressed the open communication I want to have with them." She also found that meeting with the teachers was a way to bond over education with her daughter. They discussed their impressions of her teachers and characteristics that they observed in each of them. A fellow Cohort 7 parent also discussed attending other types of educational events like the VIPS academies. She said, "I try taking off the time to be at the meetings. . . . Like this weekend [at the VIPS Saturday Academy] I need to be out of town . . . but I had to be here because I definitely don't want to miss this opportunity and all the information that we are going to receive." Parents from various cohorts consistently reported their commitment to attending school events and increasing their frequency of engaging with teachers and counselors.

Several parents discussed their involvement with their children's academic and professional pursuits. In some cases they offered emotional support more than they did direct academic assistance. One mother described her interaction with her 11th-grade daughter. She said:

> Well, I don't really help her with her homework, but what I do is sit with her; I'll keep her company. If she's reading something in English, she'll run ideas by me; we'll talk about it. "Oh, Mum, what do you think?" you know. I don't tell her what to do, but I offer feedback. She's in art AP also, AP chemistry. And so just being there, I think, just being a presence is helpful. Just to be in the room with her while she's doing her homework helps sometimes. And she seems to like that.

Several parents also discussed how they support their children's academics through the pro-education, pro-college conversations that they have and their willingness to identify academic resources and opportunities within their communities. A Cohort 6 parent spoke of a daughter who is interested in science and medicine. She sought out a volunteer opportunity for her at a hospital. She said, "She's volunteered at Kaiser Hospital in the lab and she's had an opportunity to explore some careers in that network with doctors and nurses." Other parents took a more active approach to their academic engagement. One such parent gave insight into her particular engagement. Her daughter was enrolled in community colleges while still in high school. She stated, "If I have to take the class with her [then] that's fine. We take it together. They [other students] don't know she's my daughter. They don't know I'm her mom. We sit there and we go through the semester." Regardless of the type of engagement, VIPS parents displayed an understanding of the important roles that parents play in their children's overall academic success.

Far too often it is said that parents of color are disinterested and not involved in their children's education. However, the behaviors that these parents exhibited offer a stark contrast with the dominant narrative that questions Black parents' commitment to the educational process. In some cases these parents became engaged, and in other cases they increased their level of engagement, through their participation in VIPS Saturday academies. The data demonstrate that Black parents used multiple methods to become involved in their children's educations, including the conversations they had about school and classwork and their involvement in education-related activities.

PARENTS DISCUSS VIPS'S IMPACT ON THEIR CHILDREN

Parent engagement is a vital piece in the VIPS paradigm, but the program is constructed to have the most impact on the students it serves. As one would expect, the parents spoke profusely of the effect that VIPS participation has had on their children. One common theme that appeared throughout the focus groups was the change that parents observed in the academic self-confidence of their children. A Cohort 7 parent commented, "The major difference I've noticed in my daughter is . . . the level of confidence. . . . Ordinarily she would shy away from new things. . . . Now she's much more assertive in terms of participating in class and in fact leading in class." Another parent observed similar growth in her son. She said:

> My son was able to do the summer program and I saw a tremendous change in him. I saw a whole new more mature man. . . . When he came home it was like his chest was up more and he was walking taller and prouder.

Still another parent witnessed similar growth in the confidence of her son. She said:

> [My son] is growing and maturing. His self-confidence is so much greater than it used to be. . . . My son comes home and tells me . . . how he's able

to share things that are going on with him [with his VIPS mentor]. . . .
VIPS has provided him with an inner strength so now he's even more
open to talking to me about things.

This increased confidence is a key component of overall academic achievement. As students begin to believe in themselves and their ability to be successful, their performance increases (Bandura, 1977).

VIPS students' increased academic self-confidence also led to them
assuming new attitudes about their schooling and adopting new pro-education
behaviors. According to the parents, VIPS participation results in a heightened
level of ownership over their academic performance. A parent commented:

I know for a fact [that] after attending the 2-week program she learned to
take initiative with her education. . . . She implemented everything she
learned immediately. She was on Associated Student Body cabinet. . . .
She's enjoys speaking publicly now. . . . She's much more confident and
she started the [VIPS] club. She wasn't in any clubs last year; she got into
this program and now she's in like four clubs.

While this parent observed new behaviors such as taking leadership
positions, founding student organizations, and speaking publicly, other parents
noticed changes in how their children approached school. A parent said:

What I noticed the most when my son came back from the summer
program was that his competitive nature as far as academics was way up.
Like he realized [he] has to do certain things to get what [he] wants and
there are students out here really competing with [one another].

Other parents noticed similar changes, particularly after students attended
the summer residential program at UCLA. Another parent observed:

I see him after last summer being so much more organized. . . . He
understands that as a result of being on this campus [UCLA] and having
to fulfill what he is here to do, that it is really his responsibility and
I think that I have seen that transition where he is really owning for
himself, that what he puts in, he gets out.

Multiple parents revealed that their children began to keep schedules, agen-
das, and files to help them stay academically organized in addition to the
parents observing an increase in extracurricular and volunteer participation.
Student experiences with VIPS, whether with mentors, at Saturday
Academies, or at the summer programs, also resulted in heightened critical

thinking and awareness of social justice issues that affect them and their communities. When responding to a question about the impact that VIPS has had on their children, one parent explained:

> One of the good things about the program . . . was the fact that there was that component of teaching how to deal with social justice [issues]. I think that's where the confidence boost may have come from. . . . They were compelled to see certain situations and deal with certain situations. . . . This program is giving those confidence boosters to the students . . . to allow them to be able to step up and speak up and stand strong.

A fellow parent echoed those sentiments when describing their child's experience. This parent remarked, "I think it is a program that offers both support and understanding about the world. . . . The social justice aspect, it has really made a huge impact on her that it has her thinking outside of herself." Many VIPS students experienced this type of awakening while in the program. Another parent said:

> But what I have been noticing about him since his involvement with the program is his interest in social justice. He came home from the 2 weeks that he spent here on campus and I think his eyes were open. And so his whole understanding of social justice and the conversations that he and I are now able to have in regards to it is just amazing. Because I think before we kind of somewhat lived in a bubble.

As has been mentioned elsewhere in this book, increased critical consciousness about and awareness of social justice issues is an expected outcome of VIPS participation.

This section thus far has outlined several of the effects that VIPS has had on student participants from the perspective of their parents. Students have demonstrated higher levels of academic self-confidence, taken greater ownership of their education, engaged in pro-education practices such as taking more rigorous courses and participating in extracurricular activities. They have also shown an increased interest in social justice and higher levels of critical consciousness. Ultimately, the hope is for these results to contribute to students' overall academic performance because the VIPS program is designed to push students to become competitive college applicants. Parents talked about their children's willingness to challenge themselves to a greater degree as a result of program participation. One parent mentioned that her daughter was "encouraged this year. She listened to her VIPS family to take three AP classes at once," something she would not have done in the past. Another parent stated, "My child is more focused. . . . She sees the importance of making sure that she's taking the right courses. She has three AP courses, and it's her making sure that she's staying on top [of her courses]." Other parents spoke more specifically about the impact the summer program had on their children's writing. When discussing her son, a Cohort 6 parent explained, "This program helped him to excel and be comfortable in English to be able to excel in it. He didn't think he could [pass] . . . but to have this family [VIPS] talk to him and push him [helped]." Improved writing was a theme among the parents. Another parent said:

> That writing class was amazing because I've already been to back-to-school night . . . and to hear the comments from his teacher on how he can just give the class a topic and my son is just running with it. Whereas before it would take him time to sit there and think like "what am I gonna write?" But now he's been given the tools because of this program.

A Cohort 6 parent described the impact the VIPS summer writing course had on her daughter. She said:

> The class in the summer was a wonderful, wonderful tool for my daughter. That English class was excellent and it has definitely taught my daughter exactly what was necessary as far as writing and being analytical and evaluating and doing all the necessary things required in writing a proper paper. That was invaluable.

VIPS seeks not only to prepare students to be competitively eligible for top universities but also to create a support system that includes parents and families throughout Los Angeles and Pasadena. VIPS has created its own network of professional parents, college-educated family members, and community partners through its Saturday Academy and Family Day events. Parents and families have come together to hold town hall meetings, parent clubs, and support groups in their schools and neighborhoods. The VIPS network spreads across the nation thanks to parent input and participation, making it easier for students to be supported wherever they may choose to attend college.

Six

University Perspectives on the Need for and Impact of Outreach Programs

Terry K. Flennaugh, Bree Blades, and Whitney Gouche

University-based outreach and recruitment programs play an important role in the educational pipeline for historically underrepresented communities of color, especially for students from low-income, urban communities. While hundreds of access programs operate in postsecondary institutions across the country, the mission of these programs and their method for creating pathways to higher education for underrepresented communities can vary in significant ways (Domina, 2009; Gándara & Bial, 2001). Given the wide range of approaches that programs adopt in an effort to create both greater access to their campuses and increased diversity in their student bodies it becomes important to situate these college access programs in a historical and contemporary context while also highlighting the crucial role college and university administrators play in the creation, sustainability, and success of these programs. This chapter will discuss the need for university-based outreach and enrichment programs and the social and political challenges they face today. Further, it will highlight the perspectives of administrators involved in the creation of UCLA's VIP Scholars program and offer recommendations for college and university stakeholders invested in creating effective models for postsecondary access for underrepresented groups at their campuses.

HISTORY OF UNIVERSITY-BASED OUTREACH AND ENRICHMENT PROGRAMS

The disparities in academic performance among students of color and low-income and first-generation students enrolled in postsecondary institutions across the nation have been well documented in educational research for many decades (Allen, 1988; Hurtado, Carter, & Spuler, 1996; Sellers, Chavous, & Cooke, 1998; Steele, Spencer, & Aronson, 2002; Strayhorn, 2010). Gloria Ladson-Billings (2006) argues that the term *achievement gap* has become part of everyday language spoken by various stakeholders. She states, "We need to look at the 'education debt' that has accumulated over time. This debt comprises historical, economic, sociopolitical, and moral components" (p. 3). While the *education debt* is not the focus of this chapter, oftentimes college access programs are charged with the task of alleviating the achievement gap as if that were a simple solution. The deeply rooted systemic and institutional racism that plagues our education system continues to impair our urban youth and hence keep us in debt.

The lack of representation of historically underrepresented and underserved students as applicants, admits, and enrollees at highly selective universities across the nation has sparked many debates about access, opportunities, and choice (Domina, 2009; Gándara & Bial, 2001; Kirst & Venezia, 2004; Oakes, 2003). While much of the research on university access focuses on access and opportunities for urban youth to attend bachelor degree–granting institutions, the following questions still remain: What roles and responsibilities do universities play in creating, sustaining, and supporting college pathways? How are urban youth of color affected when urban pre-K–12 schools and colleges/universities fail to develop meaningful partnerships? The educational debt belongs to everyone; government, K–12 schools, and colleges are all responsible for investment in our youth. Heller's (2011) work, *The States and Public Higher Education Policy: Affordability, Access, and Accountability,* is divided into three sections that pertain to higher education: accountability, access, and accountability. Within each section, various authors discuss relevant topics. Patrick Callan's chapter titled "Reframing Access and Opportunity: Public Policy Dimensions," addresses the systemic and institutional changes that need to occur in order to establish an equitable educational playing field. Callan states, "Colleges have been quick to criticize high schools for poorly prepared students and for subsequent low college completion rates but slow to address their own responsibilities for college readiness" (p. 100). Subsequently, Callan implies that institutions and states need to make commitments to college access; hence, college readiness is a statewide policy issue that must be systematically designed and implemented through standards, curriculum assessments, and teacher training.

Unfortunately, because of the amount of resources needed at K–12 schools, primary and secondary education simply cannot independently tackle institutional issues that substantially affect college access. There is an utter lack of understanding of how historical, economic, and sociopolitical factors affect the educational experiences of African American and Latino students. Furthermore, policymakers do not grasp how those experiences influence and perpetuate the preexisting structural and institutional barriers developed at the college level. The need for state policy and university partnerships are more prominent now than they have ever been because of the notion people have about living in a postracial "color blind" society. A substantial number of notable court cases (e.g., *Regents of the University of California v. Bakke* [1978], *Grutter v. Bollinger* [2003], and *Fisher v. University of Texas* [2013]) highlight some of the arguments individuals have presented to the Supreme Court about the use of affirmative action in college admission policies. It is evident that many remain ignorant about the systemic racism that occurs in all facets of life, especially in the educational system, which serves as a precursor for other environments presenting challenges individuals may encounter later in life. States such as California, Michigan, Texas, and Washington are notorious for their initiatives prohibiting affirmative action in public education. It is unfortunate that admission policies and recruitment strategies will continue to serve as gatekeepers against marginalized groups because of a lack of awareness, understanding, and willingness to engage in critical dialogue about the college process.

The presence of first-generation, low-income students at degree-granting universities is steadily increasing for all racial groups; however, students of color graduate at lower rates than those of their White counterparts. According to the National Center for Education Statistics, 43% of first-time, full-time, bachelor degree–seeking White students at 4-year postsecondary institutions who started in 2007 graduated within 4 years, in comparison with 20% and 29% for Black and Latino students, respectively. Traditionally, students of color have been disproportionately underrepresented during the entire college process. While pursuing postsecondary education during the first half of the 20th century was a privilege for the middle and upper class, currently the United States cannot afford to reward some and exclude many and compete globally. Because of demographic and economic shifts, the federal government focused on providing resources and support for this new wave of first-generation, low-income students who were historically omitted from postsecondary institutions. Callan suggests, "Government policies supported higher education as a means to address a wide range of larger national public issues, problems, and purposes like industrialization and the avoidance of large-scale postwar unemployment; competition for scientific and technological superiority during the Cold War; the moral imperatives of equity and civil rights; the encouragement of the national, state, and regional economic growth; and the promotion of social mobility" (Heller, 2011, p.

88). Furthermore, Swail and Perna (2002) state, "The federal approach to increasing access to colleges has historically focused on making need-based aid available to students through the Pell Grant, campus-based, and subsidized- and unsubsidized-loan programs" (p. 18). Affordability has always been an integral part of the college process, especially as it relates to access, choice, persistence, and completion. However, the federal government's approach to increasing college access for disadvantaged students through financial aid will not solve the inequalities that exist in the pre-K–20 educational system. In order to strengthen the educational pipeline for first-generation, economically disadvantaged students, federal, state, and local governments must establish partnerships and policies to better assist the precollegiate academic outreach programs and interventions that provide support for students.

Many college outreach programs have similar programmatic components that encourage students and support them in pursuing postsecondary education. Tierney and Hagedorn (2002) have identified eight components college access programs should incorporate when designing and implementing a program that serves underrepresented populations: mentorship, college and career preparation, peer groups, college counseling and advising, financial assistance, culturally relevant curriculum, family involvement, and building strong partnerships with colleges. These are vital in strengthening and sustaining any college outreach program. Each component has an integral part to play in the college process because each interaction provides students and parents/guardians with a wealth of information and resources to aid in matriculating into college successfully. The hidden curriculum of higher education is not so easily accessible to first-generation, low-income students who are not traditionally deemed to possess the social, cultural, and economic capital to enroll in, persist at, and complete college. Oftentimes, many college access programs serve as the only source of college knowledge because of the lack of resources and personnel at school sites. There are many college choice models that examine the experiences students encounter as they pursue a postsecondary education.

As discussed in Chapter 2, the Hossler and Gallagher (1987) college choice model divides the college process into three phases: predisposition, search, and choice. The predisposition phase focuses on students' decision to further their education beyond their high school career. This phase is important because there are various stakeholders that unconsciously or consciously play an integral part in a student's decision to attend college. Often, students' perceptions of self are based on their academic capabilities, which are influenced by their social identities and the support, or lack thereof, of their family and peers. During the search phase, students acquire knowledge about individual colleges and begin to identify information like learning environment and campus life that is relevant to their interest. Last, the choice phase is a comprehensive process because it encompasses the values, beliefs, and experiences of students that shape their decision to enroll at a particular college. Most college outreach programs are designed to walk students through the entire college process as outlined in the Hossler and Gallagher model. However, there are a limited number of programs that empower and liberate students of color and encourage them to actively engage with the education system and within their communities to become agents of change.

Federal Programs

In the midst of the civil rights movement, President Lyndon B. Johnson signed Public Law 88-452, also known as the Economic Opportunity Act (EOA) on August 20, 1964. The goal of the act was to provide all citizens with "the opportunity for education and training, the opportunity to work, and the opportunity to live in decency and dignity." During the civil rights movement, the federal government established numerous programs and policies to improve economic and educational opportunities especially for marginalized communities. According to Alexander (2010), "As the Civil Rights Movement began to evolve into a 'Poor People's Movement,' it promised to address not only Black poverty, but White poverty as well—thus raising the specter of a poor and working-class movement that cut across racial lines" (p. 39). As a direct response to the Economic Opportunity Act, the executive office established the Office of Economic Opportunity to funnel and mobilize all programs that were established through the War on Poverty into the Office of Economic Opportunities. Upward Bound became the first federally funded precollegiate program that originated from the Early Opportunity Act. According to the U.S. Department of Education (2015), "Upward Bound serves: high school students from low-income families; and high school students from families in which neither parent holds a bachelor's degree." The services include tutoring, educational counseling, and cultural enrichment; however, all Upward Bound projects must provide instruction in math, laboratory science, composition, literature, and foreign language during their after-school, Saturday, and summer programs (U.S. Department of Education, 2015). There are about 900 Upward Bound programs operating at 2- and 4-year postsecondary institutions throughout the United States. Despite Upward Bound being the first federally funded precollege program administered by the Department of Education, there is a lack of research on summative evaluations that capture the effectiveness of the program.

Shortly after passage of the Early Opportunity Act, President Johnson signed the Higher Education Act of 1965 to "strengthen the educational resources of our colleges and universities and to provide financial assistance for students in postsecondary and higher education." With a substantial number of students enrolling in postsecondary institutions, the Department of Education created another federally funded precollegiate program to support underrepresented groups. Similar to Upward Bound, Talent Search encourages students to pursue a postsecondary education; however, Talent Search also provides support for students who want to reenroll in secondary and postsecondary educational programs. In 1990, a longitudinal study was conducted at the University of Tennessee at Knoxville to better understand the effect of Talent Search on student participants from 1980 through 1989 (Brewer & Landers, 2005). Its authors found that Talent Search was beneficial to the student participants when compared with nonparticipants. However, they identified the 10-year time span between the date of the study and the date of students' participation in the program as a limitation of the study. As with Upward Bound, there is insufficient research to evaluate Talent Search.

In 1968, Student Support Services, formally Special Services for Disadvantaged Students, became the first federally funded program to provide programming and services for students who enrolled in college during the first reauthorization of the Higher Education Act. Upward Bound, Talent Search, and Student Support Services were called TRiO programs. After the eighth reauthorization of the Higher Education Act, in 1998, Gaining Early Awareness and Readiness for Undergraduate Programs (GEAR UP) were developed. Although GEAR UP is not a part of the original TRiO programs, it provides similar precollege resources and support to underrepresented student groups through a cohort model serving approximately one million middle and high school students. GEAR UP is unique in design because it requires a dollar-to-dollar in-kind donation from community partnerships. Regardless of the mission and method used by precollegiate outreach programs, the need to create college pathways and opportunities for underrepresented groups is the main objective. The effectiveness of federally funded college access programs has been difficult to document because of the lack of evaluations of college access programs (Gándara & Bial, 2001). It is undeniable that college access programs affect the lives of many students, but student participation in programs does not always correlate to high school graduation, college matriculation, and graduation.

State-System Partnerships

As previously mentioned, institutional commitment coupled with state policy plays a vital role in improving college access and opportunities. In

California, for example, the Early Academic Outreach Program (EAOP), formally known as Partnership, was established in 1976 at UC Berkeley. The UC system aimed to address the educational needs of the state of California by implementing EAOP across all 10 campuses. According to Cooper, Jackson, Azmitia, Lopez, and Dunbar (1995), "The program's main goals were to inform students and their parents of UC entrance requirements and to support students' academic achievement" (p. 3). The program focused on providing academic services for underrepresented students of color and first-generation low-income students, which would increase the amount of UC eligible students and with time increase the number of UC applicants and graduates. Quigley (2002) identified the three core components of EAOP as preparation services, achievement services, and enrichment services. Another systemwide initiative that is partially funded by the California Department of Education is the Early Assessment Program (EAP). EAP was designed to "provide opportunities for students to measure their readiness for college-level English and mathematics in their junior year of high school, and to facilitate opportunities for them to improve their skills during their senior year" (Early Assessment Program, n.d.). Howell and colleagues (2010) outlined three tasks of EAP: identify students' college preparedness during the 11th grade, collaborate with high school partnerships, and provide 12th-grade interventions. California's three-tier higher education system is highly respected across the nation because of its plan to increase college enrollment and graduation. Although innovative in 1960, California's Master Plan for higher education has left behind many students because they are not eligible for the Cal State or UC system or they are unaware of the admissions process.

Campus Programs

On July 28, 1967, President Johnson established the National Advisory Commission on Civil Disorder in response to the racial uprising that occurred during the 1960s in many cities across the nation. The 11-member commission investigated 23 cities to identify the socioeconomic challenges African Americans experienced through racial discrimination. A report by Barbara A. Rhodes (1971) provides resources and insights about the High Potential Program. Rhodes notes that the commission emphasized that "education in a democratic society must equip children to develop their potential and to participate fully in American life" (p. 4). Considering the historical times, former UC president Charles Hitch issued a report to the Board of Regents on May 17, 1968, to address institutional racism in the educational system at large but more specifically within the UC system. The Black Students and United Mexican American Students Union, and faculty, staff, and administrators at UCLA worked together to address the admission practices that excluded underrepresented students at UCLA. Eager to challenge the institutional inequalities and inequities that existed at UCLA, students established the High Potential Program. Rhodes (1971) states, "The High Potential Program is an attempt to engage the underprivileged Afro-American and Chicano in higher education and to have them return to their communities and participate meaningfully and effectively in their uplift" (p. 4). Essentially, the High Potential Program provided access and opportunities to students who possessed an abundance of community cultural wealth and assets that were not traditionally captured in the admissions process. Initially the High Potential Program focused on three areas: student entry programs, curriculum expansion and improvements, and urban research and problem solving. Prior to 2001 when UC Berkeley adopted the holistic and comprehensive process from the Ivy League schools, the High Potential Program encouraged UCLA to recognize and validate the wealth of knowledge students possess that remained untapped in the educational system at large.

Despite the significant gains made by the High Potential Program the university synthesized various aspects of the program into the Academic Advancement Program (AAP) to expand access and opportunities for underrepresented groups. AAP aims to create academic programs, provide academic support, and promote access for potential UCLA matriculants. Eager to strengthen relationships with underserved communities throughout the greater Los Angeles area, the Afrikan Student Union developed Students Heightening Academic Performance through Education (SHAPE) in 1995. SHAPE was established as a response to Standing Policy 1, a decision made by the UC Board of Regents to ban the use of race, ethnicity, and gender in the admissions process. Initiated and run by students, SHAPE aims "to increase the access of underrepresented students in higher education through student empowerment, holistic development, and the raising of Afrikan consciousness" (UCLA Community Programs Office, 2016). Additionally, through tutoring, advising, counseling, fieldtrips, and leadership trainings, urban youth are encouraged to pursue postsecondary education and supported in their efforts. The High Potential Program was pivotal in the process to increase recruitment, retention, and representation of a diverse population at UCLA. In 1968, that program admitted "50 Blacks, 48 Chicanos, 1 Puerto Rican, and 1 Costa Rican," none of whom met traditional UCLA admission requirements (Rhodes, 1971, p. 13). The program was a catalyst for other outreach programs that targeted underserved groups in Los Angeles County. The efforts and dedication of UCLA undergraduate students, faculty, and staff members played a significant role in altering university recruitment and admission practices.

CHALLENGES FACED BY UNIVERSITY-BASED OUTREACH AND ENRICHMENT PROGRAMS

Despite the benefits college access programs produce for students and universities, these programs face significant challenges that prohibit their scalability and success. Many challenges these programs face stem from racialized and financial debates that question both their fairness and necessity. Debates surrounding postracialism, meritocracy, and finances often ignore disadvantages students of color and low-income students face when they try to gain access to higher education, while simultaneously posing multifaceted challenges for college access programs that intend to bring awareness to these disadvantages and assist students in combating them.

One of the challenges faced by college access programs is navigating within an institution that has adopted postracial or color blind ideologies. Claims of living in a postracial society often justify race blind admissions practices while a blind eye is turned to the racialized disadvantages and challenges students of color face when pursuing higher education. The disproportionately low rates of minority student enrollment in postsecondary education compared with those of White students and recent racialized incidents on numerous campuses across the United States illustrate that a postracial society is merely an ideology, not a reality. Students of color often experience a hostile and racialized campus climate in which they are discriminated against, ostracized, targeted, and harassed (Museus, Ravello, & Vega, 2011). Not only does the concept of living in a postracial society affect campus climate; it also affects admission opportunities. Believing that we live in a postracial society and eliminating race-based admissions practices indicate to some that students from all racial backgrounds are provided equal opportunity to become academically strong applicants. Racial disparities that affect the postsecondary outcomes for students of color are simply ignored. Administrators, faculty, and even students adopt the idea that the best students are admitted because of their hard work. The postracial society mindset ignores institutionalized and systemic racism embedded in admissions policies, practices, and college preparation that puts students of color at a disadvantage, a disadvantage that few who have the power to make change, such as senior level administrators, understand or recognize (Howard & Flennaugh, 2011). Quaye, Griffin, and Museus (2015) posit that "some aspects of campus cultures are so deeply embedded in the organization fabric of institutions and taken for granted by their members that people within these campuses never reflect on and do not completely understand these cultural elements and how they impact students of color" (p. 27). College access programs and the students who participate in them often face adversity because of this concept. Administrators at various campuses struggle with the justification for funding programs that are geared to serve a racially targeted population. In a postracial society, programs like these are deemed unnecessary because race is believed to no longer be a discriminating factor in admissions, despite the continuous low enrollment of students of color compared with that of White students.

Further, college access programs may come under scrutiny from administrators who question the legality and fairness of race-targeted programs. After the elimination of affirmative action, through dictates holding race-based admissions policies illegal, programs that target students based on race face legal scrutiny because they are seemingly providing an advantage for students of color while disadvantaging or discriminating against White students. Administrators may argue that programs like these are unfair because they discriminate against students, particularly White students, who do not meet certain racial criteria by denying them additional resources and support.

College access programs face a lack of stable and increasing financial support to encourage and scale the work they are doing. A decision of whether or not to financially support college access programs is an indication of federal, state, and institutional priorities. Federally funded programs like GEAR UP, Talent Search, and Upward Bound have seen no substantial increases in funding over the past decade. In fact, in this period all these programs have experienced a more than 10% budget cut if you compare their highest fiscal year budget with their budget of fiscal year 2014–2015.[2] Although programs such as TRiO, Upward Bound, and GEAR UP have experienced budget cuts over the past decade, the government is held responsible for the longevity of these programs and for the support of the students they serve so the budget has some stability. However, the challenges of securing funding at the state and even institutional level, especially for smaller programs like VIP Scholars, become a little nuanced because individual state institutions do not have the same federal obligation that requires programming geared toward a specific demographic. Securing funds to support college access programs at the state level proves to be a more complex and challenging issue because states have more autonomy over their budgets and often do not prioritize funding for these programs. For example, in a newsletter published by UCLA's Early Academic Outreach Program (EAOP), the director of EOAP described trends in budget uncertainty, stating, "Unfortunately, the $19.3 million that supports the University of California's academic preparation programs—including EAOP—was not included in the budget. UC's

---

2. For funding data for Upward Bound, Talent Search, and GEAR UP, see U.S. Department of Education: www2.ed.gov/programs/gearup/funding.html; www2.ed.gov/programs/triotalent/funding.html; www2.ed.gov/programs/trioupbound/funding.html.

academic preparation programs have faced this same budget uncertainty for the past four years and each year funding has been restored at the 11th hour" (UCLA Early Academic Outreach Program, 2007, p. 3). The director further explained that the community had to advocate for the funding to be included in the budget by contacting the governor and state legislature to encourage them to reinstate the funding for the program. After several revisions of the budget, funding for the academic preparation programs were included in final revisions, but not prioritized in initial drafts of the state's budget.

Historically, institutionalized college culture has catered to the elite class and posits that students who are admitted to, attend, and excel at these institutions do so as a result of their own merit (Kezar, Walpole, & Perna, 2015), an attitude that poses a challenge for college access programs. Another issue that the programs face is the institutional culture of meritocracy, which plays into racial climate. The notion of meritocracy often ignores additional resources that students from privileged backgrounds are afforded that contribute to their academic "merit." Most important, meritocracy ignores systemic and institutionalized racism and classism that increasingly disadvantage low-income students and students of color by fostering a structure that ultimately rewards the privileged while denying the obstacles that students from disadvantaged backgrounds face that impede their educational success. A controversial debating point concerning Proposition 209 and race-based admissions policies was that students who were not as qualified were getting admitted to top-performing institutions over students who were seemingly more qualified. Administrators, students, and faculty developed dissenting attitudes, specifically toward students of color, who they determined only got admitted to an institution because of the color of their skin and not because of their qualifications. Despite the fact that raced-based admissions policies have been banned in numerous states and despite the disproportionately low number of students of color enrolling at prestigious universities, the aftermath of these policies creates a hostile environment for students of color (Solórzano, Ceja, & Yosso, 2000). A recent example of this debate occurred when a law professor at UCLA released a report that suggested the holistic admissions review process illegally considers race, resulting in Black students with significantly lower scores being admitted over students with higher scores (Lott, 2014). Despite alarmingly low numbers of enrollments for students of color, particularly Black students, who make up only about 4% of UCLA enrollment, widespread opinions such as these imply that Black students are undeserving of their admissions to prestigious institutions. These statements also create hostile and unwelcoming environments for students of color whose qualifications are questioned by not only faculty but also peers. Students of color encounter White students who view them as inferior because they believe they were given a handout and downplay these students' merit. A racialized, hostile campus climate poses numerous challenges for college access programs operating at these campuses and for the students who participate in them. Those involved in college access programs catering to students of color are aware of the nuances faced by these students and the disadvantages the students face, often coming from urban school districts lacking the resources to foster a college-going environment. College access programs often act as a supplement, providing resources necessary for students coming from disadvantaged backgrounds. Students of color participating in college access programs are stigmatized because participation in such programs often goes against the ideology of meritocracy, which holds that hard work and dedication should be why students are admitted, claims that additional assistance is unfair, and questions the work ethic and intelligence of students of color.

THE CREATION OF VIP SCHOLARS

Given the previously mentioned context for historically marginalized students of color on UCLA's campus, two administrators in the office of the executive vice chancellor and provost and the Academic Advancement Program (AAP) sought to create a pipeline program to increase campus diversity. Motivated by a disturbingly low number of Black students in the UCLA freshmen cohort of 2004, then vice provost and dean Judith Smith and AAP director Adolfo Bermeo decided to take action by recruiting the services of Phyllis Hart, a retired Los Angeles–area educator with a longstanding reputation of advocating for educational justice for marginalized communities. Noting that "it was really just a belief that we had reached the bottom and there was no way out of it," Smith described how she, Bermeo, and Hart strategized possible actions to address the low enrollment of Black students despite the legal limitations of Proposition 209 and a palatable climate of fear among administrators and other personnel on campus. The first step, Smith said, was establishing justification for targeting students of color. Because UCLA had federally funded undergraduate TRiO support services and research programs that specifically target underrepresented student populations (i.e., students of color, students from low-income backgrounds, and first-generation college students), Smith, Bermeo, and Hart began to make the case that the existence of these programs on campus enabled them to target high school students in diverse urban communities who could eventually become participants upon acceptance into UCLA. Smith recalled how then UCLA chancellor Albert Carnesale was "determined that [UCLA] would not do things that were unlawful" and how the chancellor's legal counsel "wasn't very supportive" of the strategy, but did feel there was some legal coverage for an initiative as long as there was a connection to the university's federally funded programs.

With some, albeit tenuous, legal coverage from the university's vantage point, the next step to be carried out primarily by Hart was to identify partnership schools in the greater Los Angeles area and to solicit their buy-in for the Vice Provost Initiative for Pre-College (VIP) Scholars program. This, however, was no easy task. Relationships with local schools were either in disrepair or nonexistent. An important fact to note is that the passage of Proposition 209 in 1996 and the subsequent chilling effect it had on universities' efforts in underserved communities throughout the state created an environment in which admissions officers were blocked from certain practices that directly attended to issues of race and community schools were suddenly ignored and neglected. The chilling effect of Proposition 209 created an atmosphere of fear, resentment, and anger for all parties. While UCLA's contact with local K–12 schools was primarily through the Office of Admissions and Relations with Schools, an unfortunate underlying tension existed. Hart was met with both reservation and hostility as she consulted with potential campus partners and local K–12 school leaders who reminded her that UCLA had "pulled out of a lot of schools" and that many schools "didn't really trust UCLA." As Smith noted, "[Hart] was really persistent . . . and basically worked really hard. . . . We were doing something they considered illegal and yet we had the backing to do it." It would take several years of general mistrust, engendered by the university's lack of consistent presence and by perceptions by schools that they were being exploited as mere research sites, for meaningful relationships to be established. Nevertheless, navigating the reality of troubled relationships both within UCLA and between the university and local K–12 schools played a vital role in the creation of the VIP Scholars program.

As a result of these efforts, the UCLA VIP Scholars program gained access to 10 high schools in the Los Angeles and Pasadena Unified School Districts. Schools were selected based on student population (schools with high percentages of students of color were prioritized) and schools' willingness to participate in this new initiative. Each school would be promised an assigned undergraduate mentors to assist in the creation and maintenance of a college-going culture at the school through group and individual college advising sessions, coordinated Buddy Days where interested students would be brought up to UCLA's campus to shadow other undergraduates, and facilitated Parent Nights where parents and community members would receive information about the college admission process and financial aid. Finally, partner schools would serve as sites for recruiting VIP Scholars where selected students would be eligible for participation in two consecutive summer programs and, if admitted to UCLA, $20,000 in scholarship support over 4 years. Schools were understandably interested and almost immediately agreed; however, behind the scenes, Smith Bermeo, and Hart struggled to find funds to support the initiative. At the beginning of the program, Smith noted "every year it was a struggle to get the funding [for the program]," and this continued for the first 3 or 4 years. Funding specifically for the scholarship that students would receive upon enrollment at UCLA was covered through existing scholarship funding streams made available through the university in compliance with the restrictions put in place by Proposition 209. It is worth noting that this financial support was committed to these VIP Scholars before it was known how successful the program would be; it was a financial commitment that Smith was willing to make in her role as vice provost. But the summer program and school site mentors are expensive and constitute the biggest line items in the program's budget. In the program's initial year, undergraduate mentors, many of whom either were alumni of these schools or were from urban schools themselves, volunteered their time every week to advise at partner schools. Bermeo would eventually find funding for training mentors and hourly pay, a practice continued by his successor, Charles Alexander, but it was clear that this was a labor of love for all staff members who consistently committed uncompensated hours of work to the program.

Despite the commitment of program staff and the buy-in from partner schools, Smith, Bermeo, and Hart intended to keep the program under the radar, fearing a still tentative university administration mindful of the potential fallout from Proposition 209. However, it is important to highlight that in spite of this climate, other key administrators on campus became fast supporters of the VIP Scholars program and with the eventual retirement of then chancellor Carnesale and the hiring of a new general counsel who was much more receptive to the initiative and who, according to Smith, "could see how we could make a case for it under current regulations," the tide slowly turned in support of the program. So much hinged on the early success of the program and when the potential of VIP Scholars became more apparent to UCLA administrators, support for the program grew. Smith recalled how the director of admissions responded after seeing early success for the program: "When he saw the quality of students in the first [admit] year . . . he was convinced that this was a program that could really help not only in the community but could help identify students who had promise who may not have applied." This administrator's buy-in, despite opposition from staff members in his own office, stands as an example of the slow process of building support that became vital for the credibility and sustainability of the program. Many challenges still exist for the program, particularly in funding. However, buy-in from both the campus community and the partnership schools has been vital.

From the perspective of key administrators who have been involved in the creation and maintenance of the VIP Scholars program since its inception, the existence of the program offers three essential benefits to UCLA's campus. The first and most obvious is that it *enriches the university's diversity.* The presence of students from marginalized communities on UCLA's campus is important for several reasons. Not only does their presence fulfill the duty of UCLA as a public institution of higher education to enroll and serve the community in which it is located, but also their presence enriches all UCLA students' collegiate experience. As one faculty member whose scholarship and courses centered on issues of race and social justice mentioned to VIP Scholars during the summer, "I cannot effectively do my job here at UCLA without students like you in my classes." The second benefit of the VIP Scholars program to the UCLA campus is that it effectively *increases the competitiveness of UCLA* to get eligible Black students to come to the university. UCLA's standing as a highly selective university meant that it was often competing with other elite universities like UC Berkeley, Stanford, and Ivy League institutions for the same small pool of highly qualified Black students. The VIP Scholars program works to increase the size of this pool and in addition, students' early exposure, the sizable scholarship money offered, and the connection they build with other VIP Scholars help to put UCLA among the top schools that students consider. The third benefit that administrators identified about the VIP Scholars was that participants had the potential to improve UCLA's standing in urban communities. As current director of the Academic Advancement Program (AAP), Charles Alexander, stated:

> I think [the VIP Scholars program] shows the university's commitment to the schools we're working with, in terms of helping students at those schools and it contributes to an environment, atmosphere, or culture in that school that attending UCLA is a possibility. So it does give off an encouraging and positive message from that standpoint.

UCLA has been largely absent from urban schools and communities for far too long. Without meaningful partnerships, compounded by Proposition 209, students from urban schools and communities were well within their rights to be resentful toward UCLA. A public university in their city had too long been unavailable and unwelcoming to them and members of their community. The prevailing promise of "work hard and you too can become a UCLA Bruin" failed to be realized by many students from these schools who were conditioned to accept that the elite university closest to where they grew up was a place they were barred from entering. Whether UCLA administrators were willing to accept the negative perception of UCLA or not, moral support for the VIP Scholars program among many administrators on campus grew over time.

RECOMMENDATIONS FOR COLLEGE AND UNIVERSITY STAKEHOLDERS

Given the previous context and experiences of administrators seeking to increase the representation of urban students of color in predominately White institutions of higher education, we offer three recommendations for college and university stakeholders looking to enact institutional change.

1. Create a Bold Vision for Inclusion and Build Community Among Campus Partners. Key to creating the VIP Scholars program was the coming together of a small group of like-minded administrators who decided to stand up for equity and diversity on UCLA's campus. Their bold vision to create a pipeline program that targeted urban students of color from the surrounding communities at a time when so many on campus (and in the state) were paralyzed by the climate of fear and resentment stemming from the passage of Proposition 209 resulted in significant changes in campus diversity and the university's standing in urban communities, but it was no easy task. Any shift in practice that seeks to challenge the dominant narrative that college admission practices are fair, or that communities of color are less represented at flagship universities like UCLA because they are less capable, will undoubtedly cause a great deal of tension. As Harro (2000) notes, we all have to be conditioned to believe that the way institutions function to benefit agent groups (White, male, wealthy, heterosexual, etc.) and marginalize target groups (communities of color, women, poor, queer, etc.) is normal and right. Hart remarked that it was "very hard" even to assert a bold vision of diversity on UCLA's campus to her peers early in the program's inception because "values that are deeply embedded in an institution like UCLA that's in the top-ranking universities in the country [aren't] easy to change." Without a bold vision that challenges the very notion of what many believe to be possible, there would be no program.

Equally important to creating a bold vision of inclusion on campus is the important and time-consuming work of building community among campus partners so they too can buy in to this vision. Hart highlighted her effort to build consensus around a concerted effort to address diversity at UCLA by speaking with more than 80 stakeholders on campus.

So even though after speaking to about 80 different people, I won't say that it changed a lot of what we did but it brought an authenticity and a trust that might not have been there otherwise. Additionally, I was conscious of the fact that I am White and that, how dare I come in and not talk to African American people who have been living in that world and I have not and not ask for their help and assistance.

According to Hart, it was especially important to reach out to undergraduate student groups and Black students on campus about a vision for creating a pipeline for Black students to UCLA. This would prove to be critical in building a broad network of support that was not confined to just administrators on campus. Ultimately, undergraduate students would be the face of the program in partner schools. This effort to create a team with a shared vision relates to the work of scholars like Harro (2000) who note the significance of *building community* as an essential step in breaking down barriers for equity.

2. Rekindle/Establish Relationships with Pre-K–12 Schools. It is undeniable that relationships that are authentically cultivated between colleges/universities and pre-K–12 schools are beneficial to the community. According to Maurrasse (2002), "Universities and colleges are equipped to contribute effectively to their local neighborhoods in many ways, academically, economically, and beyond" (p. 3). The dominant narrative suggests that institutions of higher education possess the cultural and social capital students from disenfranchised communities need to matriculate into their institutions. However, these students possess a wealth of knowledge that would serve as a strength and asset for many campuses. Most institutions have departments or offices that are dedicated to establishing meaningful relationships with community partners, especially the local education agencies. These partnerships benefit the students, districts, schools, and colleges as well. It is imperative that colleges engage with local schools, specifically those that serve underrepresented students, because of the untapped talent within the community. Furthermore, providing students with the necessary tools and resources to pursue admission to, enroll at, and graduate from institutions of higher education is a must. Oftentimes, the admissions office recruits from feeder high schools that have a history of producing academically strong candidates. These recruits also go to local high schools to present information that is relevant to the college admissions process; however, many do not understand the culture of the school or the students' realities. For example, Hart mentioned that she was "outraged at the practices and policies that schools and districts had that systematically eliminated many African American students to get into a college access and college preparation track and on to college." Lacking a college counselor, rigorous college preparatory courses, access to college courses, and other structures and strategies that typically help pave college pathways for students, many low-income students and students of color have historically found their way blocked.

Establishing partnerships across the educational pipeline allows for critical dialogue to occur among various stakeholders. In this way college campuses would have a better understanding of the realities students encounter that disrupt their path to college. Primary and secondary schools should not be solely held responsible for establishing a college-going culture; local universities and colleges should provide resources and tools to better prepare not only students but also teachers and administrators. Despite the efforts of official college recruiters, many talented, high-potential candidates go unnoticed because the student may not be an ideal candidate based on a low grade point average or scores on other quantitative measurements that are used to assess a student's college readiness. Programs like VIPS are crucial on college campuses because they reach out to schools that may have been historically underserved and overlooked by local universities. Smith recalled Hart being adamant about serving the Pasadena Unified School District because UCLA had abandoned the schools. Considering that UCLA and Pasadena are approximately a 30-minute drive apart, UCLA did not have many students from the Pasadena Unified School District, not because there were not eligible applicants but because UCLA had become this dream school that was deemed unattainable by many of its students. The college access programs that were present in the schools did not do outreach to "average students," and their presence in the schools was limited, which was not helpful, given the high teacher and administrator turnover rate of many schools. The current director of VIP Scholars, Dr. Jonli Tunstall, stated that there was "a mistrust of UCLA, a mistrust of [college access] programs because they come in and out"; the lack of consistency and commitment made it challenging for the VIP Scholars program because there was a history of programs being removed from the schools.

Institutions that are seeking to increase the representation of students of color must invest the same if not more resources into urban communities that they invest in feeder schools. It is not uncommon for students of color to feel unwelcome, intimidated, or out of place when they visit degree-granting institutions. In a report compiled by the Consortium for the Advancement of Private Higher Education, 21 community partners shared with the Council of Independent Colleges key elements that constitute a good community–campus partnership (Leiderman, Furco, Zapf, & Goss, 2002). One recommendation outlined in the report suggests that community–campus partnerships need to "learn how to talk together about racial, ethnic, and economic inequalities and their causes with candor, and incorporate those discussions into community/campus partnership-building work" (p. 16). A lack of dialogue followed by inaction hinders the opportunity for community–college partnerships to flourish. If institutions of higher education are seeking to increase student diversity, institutions must be willing to engage in critical dialogue about challenges communities are encountering, not only to listen but also to build trust.

3. Analyze and Understand the Effects of Institutional Campus Culture on Urban Students. As institutions increase student diversity, the campus culture that favors Eurocentric ideals and privileges White, affluent males is not diversifying (Harper & Quaye, 2015). Urban students, such as students of color and low-income students, enter college with different cultural backgrounds and forms of capital than those of their predominately White and affluent peers (Perna & Titus, 2005). Institutional cultural norms, inside and outside the classroom, tend to value cultural and economic capital that these groups often lack. Thus, urban students are faced with the challenge of navigating a culture that favors certain capital, without having the appropriate resources to do so (Kezar, Walpole, & Perna, 2015). Commonly, institutional norms indicate that individual effort determines student success; however, this ideology assumes that all students have the structure and ability to engage on similar levels in order to be successful (Kezar, Walpole, & Perna, 2015). These institutional norms often ignore the social, economic, and cultural disadvantages urban students face when trying to attain success at flagship universities; the racialized and culturally demoralizing experiences of these students often go unnoticed or are handled badly and are further barriers to recruitment. To ensure that all students have equitable college experiences and success, faculty, administrators, and trustees should intentionally analyze how campus culture affects urban students on their campuses and determine the most effective way to revamp institutional culture in a way that supports success for diverse student populations.

Institutions should take responsibility for fostering an environment that allows different cultural perspectives and norms to contribute to the institutional culture. To engender a more equitable campus culture, hiring practices for faculty should include a cultural awareness component so faculty are mindful of students they are teaching in their classroom and engage them accordingly; administrators should engage in campus culture studies and develop strategies and solutions based on data; institutions should develop a campus cultural task force composed of students from different racial, ethnic, and socioeconomic backgrounds in order understand how current campus culture, embedded in racist and classist structures, directly affects student experiences and performance.

Faculty play a huge role in sustaining campus culture through how they engage with students. Tierney (2000) suggests that for educators to be most engaging and effective, they must "come to terms with the backgrounds and forces that have shaped those individuals who sit in [their] classes" (p. 11). Faculty hiring practices and tenure processes should encompass an assessment of how faculty understand student compositional diversity, and how their understanding would affect the way they teach and engage students. This assessment would allow for department deans and chairs to understand if and how faculty recognize the manner in which the cultural differences of their students influence their content and pedagogy. Department deans and chairs can use this assessment to encourage faculty to develop curricula that reflect and engage diverse backgrounds in order to influence academic success and persistence for these students (Harper, 2009).

Additionally, campus administration should be engaged in campus culture research in order to identify and understand how culture affects underrepresented students. Quaye, Griffin, and Museus (2015) posit that "some aspects of campus cultures are so deeply embedded in the organization fabric of institutions and taken for granted by their members that people within these campuses never reflect on and do not completely understand these cultural elements and how they impact students of color" (p. 27). Engaging in campus culture research will help administrators understand how institutional norms disadvantage particular groups. Administrators can use this information to develop strategies or policies that respond to the needs of multiple students.

Last, to transform institutional culture, institutions must examine the perspectives and opinions of students who experience and are affected by institutional norms. Underrepresented students must be consulted and engaged at institutional functions so that administrators can develop the best strategies and policies to serve these students (Harper, 2012). Administrators should develop an ongoing student task force that would report to executive administrators or the board of trustees to provide recommendations on what institutions can do to transform college culture in order to best meet the needs of all students.

CONCLUSION

We are not under any illusion that creating effective pathways for students from marginalized communities to intuitions of higher education is somehow easily accomplished in places where addressing issues of race, educational access, and social justice particularly for urban communities of color remains politically polarizing and prohibitively taboo. The university context for the VIP Scholars program was, and remains, complicated and elements are uncooperative at times in the larger goal of increasing the representation of ethnically and economically diverse students. However, strong leadership, political acumen, concerted efforts at consensus building, and ultimately a strong commitment to doing what's right has created a program with proven success at an institution that seemed to have insurmountable barriers. The work can be done, and it desperately needs to be done.

Seven

Postsecondary Pathways

Michelle Smith and Tr'Vel Lyons

For nearly a decade, the VIP Scholars, or VIPS, program has not wavered from its initial focus: to aid underrepresented youth from the greater Los Angeles area in achieving their dream of becoming competitively eligible for top-tier institutions of higher education. The preceding chapters have detailed the components of the VIP Scholars program, which work in concert to ensure that the primary purpose of the program—college access—is accomplished. In this chapter, we have three areas of focus. First, we address the matriculation of VIP Scholars since the program's inception. It is vital that we share these successes to demonstrate that through various approaches, the goal of college attainment is being met by leaps and bounds. We also illuminate the experiences of VIP Scholars within their undergraduate programs. Notwithstanding the scholars' success, program evaluation research has revealed areas of growth for the program that would ensure that future scholars experience comparable outcomes. We discuss areas of growth that we believe will broaden the program's scope and enable further student success. These areas include expanding alumni support, increasing STEM focus, and earlier outreach for significantly underrepresented subgroups. The second focus of this chapter emphasizes that while the program is garnering success, there is a need for expansion if it is to substantially increase the number college graduates from communities of color. Finally, we propose what can be achieved beyond the reach of the VIP Scholars program to address college access on a national level for underrepresented student populations. The final section of the chapter offers a set of recommendations and roles that multiple stakeholders, such as universities, communities, and legislators, can play in expanding college access nationwide.

NATIONAL COLLEGE MATRICULATION

The National Center for Education Statistics reports that the overall percentage of high school graduates matriculating into postsecondary institutions has steadily increased over the past 3 decades; however, there remains a significant disparity between the numbers of historically underrepresented students of color and their White and Asian counterparts (Aud et al., 2013). While the racial disparities between Black and White high school graduates who enter college immediately after completing high school have decreased, there is a significant gap based on socioeconomic status (Aud et al., 2013). Despite this trend, it is important that the influence of race on socioeconomic outcomes is considered. The Children's Defense Fund (2014) reports that a greater proportion of Black (38%) and Latino (30%) children under 18 live in poverty when compared to their White counterparts. Given these outcomes, it is vital that attention is focused on ensuring that low-income students of color have access to postsecondary institutions in an effort to increase their life opportunities. Further, the poverty data (Children's Defense Fund, 2014) demonstrate that concentrating solely on socioeconomic status when addressing access to postsecondary education is insufficient and data disaggregated by race and socioeconomic status are needed to more succinctly paint a picture of student outcomes.

Our goal as a program is to increase the number of *competitively eligible* underrepresented students for admission to selective 4-year universities. Nationwide, Black and Latino students are overrepresented at 2-year institutions and a significantly growing number attend for-profit institutions (Aud et al., 2013). In California, for example, African American high school graduates continue to be underrepresented in public 4-year universities; however, they are overrepresented in for-profit colleges (Valliani, Siqueiros, & Dow, 2013). While for-profit colleges increase access to postsecondary education by providing an additional route to college, they do very little to address the concern of providing access to an affordable public education. In California, first-time students who attended for-profit institutions borrowed at an alarmingly greater rate compared with their counterparts attending public and private nonprofit schools (Valliani et al., 2013).

Lynch, Engle, and Cruz (2010) describe for-profit institutions as luring students into pursuing "high-cost degree programs that have little chance of leading to high-paying careers, and saddle the most vulnerable students with more debt than they could reasonably manage to pay off, even if they do graduate" (p. 7). Within 2 years of entering repayment, nearly 10% of students attending for-profit schools default on their student loans and by the 3rd year 19% are in default (Lynch, Engle, & Cruz, 2010). With the vast number of low-income students of color attending these schools, it is likely that many of these students are at a greater risk for defaulting. For students who go into default without completing their degrees, the damage can be longstanding given consequences such as losing eligibility for additional aid, wage garnishment, and lowered credit scores (U.S. Department of Education, 2015). Lynch, Engle, and Cruz (2010) liken the practices of for-profit colleges and their student outcomes to those of the subprime lending industry, which led to a disastrous collapse of the economy. They note that 4-year for-profit institutions have significantly lower 6-year graduate rates (22%), with nonprofit public and private universities graduating more than twice that proportion of their students.

Despite state and national matriculation rates, VIPS cohort students have successfully enrolled at numerous 4-year colleges and universities nationwide. Many of the scholars attend 4-year colleges in California, an achievement that continues to elude many students of color throughout the state. The follow section further emphasizes the postsecondary outcomes of the program's scholars.

VIP SCHOLARS STUDENT OUTCOMES

Approximately 210 VIP Scholars cohort students have completed the program and graduated from high school since the program's inception in 2006. Among this group, over 95% were accepted by and enrolled in 4-year universities upon graduation. A significant proportion of these scholars attend public universities (76%), namely, those within the University of California and California State University systems. Approximately 105 students from Cohorts 1–7 were offered admission into the University of California, Los Angeles, which accounts for nearly 51% of the cohort students served. Among these students are Saturday Academy students who were also offered admission to UCLA; efforts to collect these data are forthcoming. Of these 105 cohort students offered admission to UCLA, 77 (73%) elected to enroll at UCLA immediately following graduation.

Given that cohort and admission years vary, there are both similarities and differences between each cohort's college admission outcomes. For example, there are cohorts that had very few students accepted by the host campus and others with over half their students offered admission. Figure 7.1 includes the percentages of scholars from each cohort who were admitted to UCLA. Note that cohort size has varied; however, there are typically 28–30 scholars who complete the program in its entirety.

Table 7.1 displays the disaggregated enrollment among cohort students who enrolled at any of the nine University of California campuses that serve undergraduates. The number of scholars who enrolled at the three most

Figure 7.1. VIPS Cohort Admit Rate (Percentage Accepted to UCLA)

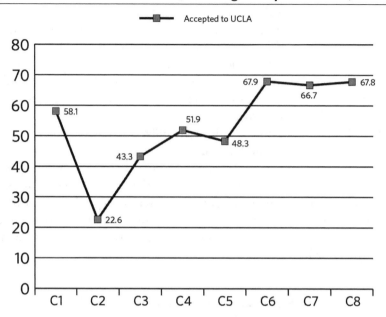

Table 7.1. University of California Enrollment by Cohort (Raw Number)

	UC School	UCLA	UC Berkeley	UC San Diego	Other UC
Cohort 1	23	15	2	2	4
Cohort 2	15	5	3	1	6
Cohort 3	14	8	2	0	4
Cohort 4	21	11	4	2	4
Cohort 5	17	11	1	0	5
Cohort 6	19	14	3	0	2
Cohort 7	20	13	3	0	4

selective UC schools (UC Berkeley, UCLA, and UC San Diego) is shown, and the remaining scholars are represented in the "Other UC" category.

Among the cohort students, six matriculated to Ivy League schools, including Yale, Harvard, and Princeton, and another four attended other prestigious private institutions such as Stanford and Northwestern. In addition to the aforementioned private schools, there are 10 VIP Scholars attending historically Black colleges and universities such as Spelman College, Morehouse College, and Tuskegee and Howard universities.

Very few of the program's scholars elect to attend community colleges or join the armed forces, likely an outcome of the program's relentless efforts to make sure that scholars complete the minimum requirements for admittance into California's public 4-year universities, which makes scholars competitive candidates for universities nationwide with comparable requirements. The Campaign for College Opportunity (Valliani et al., 2013) reports that among the 28,078 African American high school graduates entering postsecondary education in fall 2012, less than a third met the minimum requirements for admittance into California's public 4-year universities. Similarly, a large proportion of Latino students in California did not meet the eligibility requirements, with only 28% completing the A-G requirements (Valliani et al., 2013). It is important to note that the minimum eligibility for UC schools differs from those in the California State University schools, thus impacting the proportion of eligible students for the state's more selective schools. This low proportion results in far fewer African Americans being represented in freshman classes at highly competitive institutions such as UCLA and UC Berkeley, because of the reduced pool of eligible applicants (Valliani et al., 2013). These outcomes are not concentrated in California.

While students nationwide are completing more rigorous coursework in high school, the National Assessment of Educational Progress (NAEP) High School Transcript Study determined specific guidelines for diploma levels (Nord et al., 2011). The "standard" diploma requires four credits in English, and three credits each in social studies, mathematics, and science. A "midlevel" diploma requires specific restrictions for the math and science courses and also requires at least 1 year of foreign language. Finally, the "rigorous" diploma requires an additional year of math that must include precalculus or higher as well as 3 years of foreign language. This study determined that fewer African American and Latino students completed the rigorous curriculum coursework in comparison with their White and Asian counterparts. Flagship universities comparable to the University of California often require the rigorous curriculum as minimum and competitively eligible admissions requirements (Nord et al., 2011). Completing a less rigorous high school curriculum may significantly, if not outright, reduce the likelihood that a student will gain admission into a selective university.

Teranishi, Allen, and Solórzano (2004) reported that the racial composition of schools was correlated with access to the educational resources necessary to ensure college preparedness and later admittance. The authors stated that those schools with greater proportions of Black and Latino students "had fewer educational resources that resulted in poorer educational preparation and fewer opportunities for higher education" (p. 2241) Some of these resources include, but are not limited to, the availability of Advanced Placement (AP) courses, experienced instructors, and adequate guidance throughout the college choice process (McDonough, 1997; Teranishi et al., 2004). The VIP Scholars program has served as a mechanism to intercede on the behalf of our scholars to make sure that they are fully informed about the college choice process, the requirements for admittance into highly selective institutions, and what steps are needed to actualize their college goals. For example, many students are encouraged to enroll in community college courses when there is a critical shortage of honors and AP courses at their schools. When students do so, they not only can increase their grade point averages but also expose themselves to the rigors of college coursework. In addition, should scholars struggle in particular courses, they are informed of which courses they should retake to increase their GPA.

Thus far, the program's relentless efforts to increase the number of competitively eligible candidates for UC have been overwhelmingly successful. This is not only because of the percentage of scholars admitted to UC schools but also because of their admittance into comparable selective institutions in addition to the host campus. The array of institutions to which scholars are offered admittance demonstrates that the program greatly expands the range of institutions for which scholars are competitive candidates. The following section highlights the college experiences of VIPS cohort students once they have completed the program and continue to pursue undergraduate studies. This section focuses attention on those attending UCLA, particularly those who remain highly involved with the program as undergraduates in various roles.

VIP Scholars College Experience

This section moves away from a focus on our scholars as high school students and delves into the experiences of the program's scholars as they persist as undergraduates. Each year, cohort scholars are asked to complete an alumni survey so that we may gain a better understanding of their college experiences after completing the program. From these surveys we learn more about how scholars fund their education, about their participation in co-curricular activities, and about their career goals. The latest alumni survey yielded 46 responses and among those 32 were current UCLA students. The following illustrates important student outcomes, including self-reported GPAs, funding sources, majors pursued, and campus participation.

Based on their responses, it is clear that many VIPS alumni are doing relatively well in college, with 8 students reporting a GPA between 3.5 and 4.0, 30 students reporting a GPA between 3.00 and 3.49, and the remaining 8 students a GPA below 3.00. VIPS alumni are enrolled in a wide range of academic majors, among them sociology, nursing, women's/gender studies, philosophy, molecular cell development biology, ethnic studies (African American and Chicana/o studies), political science, and psychology.

Through the alumni surveys, we learned that a significant proportion of the cohort students fund their education through scholarships and grants. Fewer than half also rely on part-time employment, work study, and loans, and approximately a quarter rely on family contributions. Figure 7.2 indicates the reported distribution of the scholars' reported funding sources.

Given the rising cost of attendance, it is not surprising that scholars must rely on a combination of financial resources to fund their education, which historically has shown that financial packages that include all forms of aid had a positive impact on enrollment trends for African American students (St. John & Noell, 1989). Further, Swail, Redd, and Perna (2003), explain that students of color and low-income students who receive financial aid are more likely to persist in college; however, increased reliance on student loans may negatively affect persistence. In light of this, it is incredibly important that the scholarship component of the program is kept intact, as merit-based scholarships and grants remain scarce. As mentioned in previous chapters, the program provides a $20,000 scholarship to admitted students who choose to study at UCLA, a sum that significantly supplements the cost of attendance.

Despite the varied financial situations that force most of the scholars to balance work and school, many are also active participants in campus organizations. The importance of undergraduate student involvement and its positive influence on student persistence is vastly supported in higher education literature (Astin, 1975; MacKay & Kuh, 1994; Pascarella & Terenzini, 1991); cohort students report mainly participating in ethnic/cultural organizations and community service activities. Scholars also report participating in undergraduate research, which may better prepare those who are interested in pursuing graduate school. This has certainly been the case for scholars who participated in undergraduate research at UCLA; many have since gone on to pursue master's and doctoral degrees since graduating. Table 7.2 illustrates campus involvement among the program's scholars.

These overall findings are similar for cohort students specifically attending UCLA, who have greater direct contact and guidance from the program. VIPS students attending UCLA have access to mentorship from the program's director and assistant director, a designated academic advisor assigned to the program, and undergraduate research opportunities provided by the program. Many students also elect to work for the program as an academic year or summer program mentor, which has inspired a number of students to pursue careers in education or to incorporate social justice into their professional/graduate studies. Eight of the survey respondents reported being accepted into graduate programs. Among those, students planned to study education, social/developmental psychology, behavioral science and health education, educational policy, cognitive psychology, or law. Students interested in pursuing

Figure 7.2. Postsecondary Funding Sources Among VIP Scholars

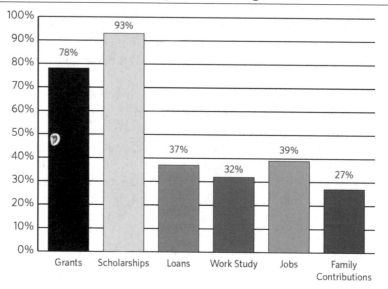

education-related programs report that the program greatly influenced their career path, especially through the mentorship they received from the program's administrative staff and the summer program faculty member. One scholar, Tristen, who has recently completed a master's program in education, shared the influence program staff had on her decision to study education:

> I never really considered entering the education field until I actually joined the VIPS program as a student in high school, so I think coming on UCLA's campus and taking the 98 Ed course with Dr. Howard, just being immersed in like the text and seeing how it's really really relevant to my life. . . . My mentors definitely had a huge role . . . helping me out, making me understand the larger problems and how everything is kind of related. . . . I eventually saw how I could be an asset to the education field or at least the things I would want to do or some of the things I could introduce to the field. (Alumni interview, 2014)

This demonstrates that the program reaches students beyond their academic endeavors and also piques their interest in addressing social justice issues in their careers. Tristen went on to discuss how her mentors, the program director, and program faculty provided invaluable mentoring to her throughout her time at UCLA. She stated,

> I think those people were very crucial. I think they all had different traits that made me gravitate towards them and I think they challenged me all

Table 7.2. Campus Involvement (Raw Number)

Activity	No Involvement	Occasional Participation	Active	Leader
Student/Campus Government	28	7	3	2
Sports (including intramural teams)	27	6	3	2
Newspaper	33	0	4	0
Undergraduate Research Programs	19	10	7	2
Performing Arts/ Music	32	3	3	0
Ethnic/Cultural Organizations	5	14	13	8
Academic/ Honors/ Professional Clubs	18	7	11	2
Internships	23	2	10	2
Community Service	6	16	14	2
Fraternity/ Sorority	31	0	2	5
Religious Club	30	3	3	2

in different ways. And I think they came in my life at a very pivotal point in my life. I think that if they had came a year later, my life would be a lot different . . . or if they came too early—I think it still would have been different.

As mentioned above, many of the UCLA students participate in undergraduate research. The program offers research opportunities to cohort students through its Research Fellows program. Cohort students elect to take a research course that focuses on completing projects related to the program. In previous years, fellows have had the opportunity to share their research at national conferences, such as the American Educational Research Association annual meeting. Throughout the years the Research Fellows course has provided students with an opportunity to learn more about the research process, including working on data collection and analysis, developing executive research reports, presenting findings to stakeholders, and writing research proposals.

In addition to following the Research Fellows course, cohort students have participated in research programs such as the McNair Research Scholars program, which is a federal TRiO program, and university-sponsored programs. Many cohort students elected to address social justice education issues for their research projects on topics such as the impact of the educational environment on gang-affiliated youth, AP opportunities in Los Angeles public schools, Black male K–12 experiences and access to postsecondary opportunities, and the impact of the small-school movement in public high schools. Through these undergraduate research programs, the scholars were given the opportunity to present their findings at a university-sponsored event. Overall, participation in undergraduate research has aided students in their becoming more competitive for graduate school admissions as well as feeling prepared for the rigor of graduate-level studies. Myles, who planned to begin a graduate program in education in fall 2015, conducted research at UCLA's Black Male Institute and shared how his work as a mentor and researcher aided him in drawing connections between research and practice. He explained, "They're scarily related or connected. Uh, I look at the number for Black males in education: the dropout rate, truancy, uh graduation, I look at all that . . . and then I go to the high school and I see it, experience it."

Given the extensive support that UCLA cohort students receive, expanding the program will allow us to broaden our reach among cohort students, especially those outside UCLA and those pursuing STEM majors. This expansion will provide the program with the means to reach a greater number of alumni students. The program hopes to maintain student success and witness marked improvement in better serving cohort students once they reach college through these expansion efforts. For undergraduate student outreach, the program seeks to develop initiatives that will target non-UCLA students and UCLA students pursuing STEM-related careers. The initiatives are described in detail below.

ALUMNI INITIATIVES

As described in the previous section, an overwhelming number of VIP Scholars who are offered admission to UCLA choose to pursue their undergraduate studies at the host campus. However, many other scholars, who attended colleges and universities nationwide, would benefit from receiving support from the program. Each year, there are approximately 60 alumni, almost 15 per cohort, who are still pursuing their undergraduate degrees at other institutions. Because of programmatic constraints, the program is unable to adequately provide support to students outside the university. The program hopes to acquire full-time staff members who will lead this initiative by serving as VIPS alumni support officers (ASOs). These professionals will serve in two primary capacities: expanded alumni outreach and STEM support initiatives.

Alumni Support

Nearly half or more of the students reported through the alumni survey that the program could support their education through academic counseling, scholarship opportunities, internship and research opportunities, and guidance with pursuing graduate school. This includes both UCLA alumni and those attending schools elsewhere. Over two-thirds (27) of the students reported interest in pursuing graduate school upon graduation and another 28% (11) were interested in professional school. Figure 7.3 displays alumni expectations concerning ways the program can better support their school experience, which could have a positive impact in their graduate and professional school preparation.

The ASOs will serve as mentors to 1st- and 2nd-year students in an effort to smooth their transition to the university. Throughout the year, an ASO will meet with each 1st-year student once a quarter to learn more about the student's academic progress and career goals. In addition, each student will submit an action plan during the fall quarter, which will guide his or her meetings throughout the year in an effort to reach the desired academic goals.

Although the ASO will work closely with 1st- and 2nd-year students, those with junior and senior standing will be connected with a graduate mentor within the university graduate mentoring office based on their career interests. These students will also meet with one of the remaining VIPS senior staff members (director, assistant director, graduate student researcher) once each quarter to discuss their progress. While the ASO will not work directly with this subset of students, he or she will provide information regarding campus-based resources available to them.

Alumni Outreach

Thus far, four cohorts of students have completed their undergraduate programs, with many from UCLA finishing within 4 years and having gone on to graduate school. While the alumni surveys are helpful, this provides only a snapshot of self-reported outcomes from those who choose to respond.

Figure 7.3. Percentage of Desirable Student Support

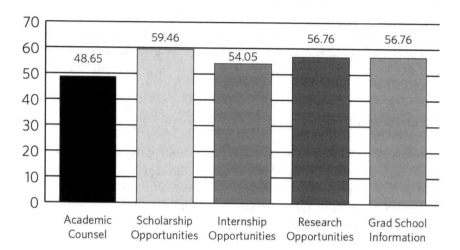

Should the program have the capacity to expand its outreach to students beyond UCLA in a systematic way, we may begin to witness outcomes similar to those at UCLA. In addition, given students experiencing significant gains through the summer program while in high school, alumni outreach will allow us to better understand our reach as a program beyond high school.

While most 4-year universities offer outreach to students interested in these programs, additional guidance from those within the program who have established a vested interest in our students' outcomes may have a significant impact. Furthermore, with our continued support, cohort students would be able to remain connected to the program in a meaningful way. The ASO would spearhead the effort to stay in close contact with students who do not attend UCLA. This aspect of the initiative would initially consist of compiling correct contact information from VIPS alumni, especially those who are enrolled in college. The ASO would also be responsible for sending out a monthly newsletter to VIPS alumni that shares resources such as information on national scholarships, internships, and graduate school. In addition, the ASO would work closely with the graduate student researcher to collect and analyze the annual alumni survey. In addition, the ASO would work closely with the program's social media committee to expand the program's social media presence as it relates to the needs of our cohort students.

Finally, the ASO is responsible for hosting a biannual VIPS reunion that will serve to bring together the growing number of alumni students and past staff, which would help to build a greater sense of community among those who have participated in the program in various capacities past and present. A biannual coming together of VIPS students and staff would not only help students remain connected to the program but also provide an opportunity to maintain and build their social networks as they progress through their careers.

STEM SUPPORT INITIATIVES

The Department of Education has developed initiatives to significantly increase the number of graduates with STEM degrees (PCAST, 2010, 2012). Although a significant focus is on K–12 education in terms of raising interest and performance in STEM areas and careers to increase the number of students who pursue majors in these areas, there remains a growing concern about student persistence in STEM majors. Because of the rigor and competitiveness of STEM majors, there are students who hope to pursue careers in STEM but often do not find the support they need to experience success in these majors. Within the program, there are students who have entered college majoring in STEM fields but later changed to non-STEM majors. Often, these students experienced feeling of isolation and sometimes self-doubt as a result of their significant underrepresentation in the major and lack of community support. Because of an underrepresentation of students of color and women in the STEM fields, the program seeks to expand in such a way that will better prepare students for the rigor of a STEM major and help them complete their respective programs once they enter college.

In previous years, the program has offered a mathematics course during the 2-week program; however, offering a course of this nature to students at various math levels has not been without its challenges. Nationwide, math and science serve as gatekeeper courses that keep students from earning standard and advanced diplomas that lead to matriculation into 4-year institutions. As mentioned in the paragraphs above, the midlevel and rigorous course curriculum is primarily determined by including advance mathematics and science coursework. This is especially so for mathematics, as the course rigor increases at each diploma type. A greater proportion of Black and Latino students who did not earn a standard diploma in comparison with their White and Asian peers solely lacked the science requirement (Nord et al., 2011). In addition to course requirements, there are institutions that require SAT Subject Test scores to determine admission into specific STEM majors, which may serve as a barrier for those scholars who do not score well on these additional measures. Programs such as TRiO's Upward Bound Math and Science program, Level Playing Field's SMASH Programs, and the

California's COSMOS summer school programs offer starting points for how the program can begin offering more STEM support.

The program seeks to move in a direction that will provide support that not only assists students in becoming more successful in advanced math *and* science while in high school but also offer enrichment to those students who express interest in pursuing STEM majors. The ASOs would also take the lead on STEM initiatives that will serve both the high school cohort students and those attending UCLA. The STEM initiative will have three subcategories: mentorship, academic preparation, and undergraduate persistence.

Mentorship

The mentorship program for the STEM initiatives would consist of selecting at least two or three undergraduate mentors who would provide mentorship to VIPS cohort students throughout the academic year. Up to two mentors would be assigned to each locale (i.e., Los Angeles and Pasadena) and host workshops at their respective schools throughout the academic year. The mentors would host at least one STEM workshop at each of their sites once an academic quarter and meet with each cohort student interested in STEM from their sites once a quarter. The STEM mentors would also develop a STEM Buddy Day, when high school students would visit the university and shadow upper-level students completing STEM majors. The culminating event for the mentoring aspect of the STEM initiative consists of the mentors hosting a STEM Saturday Academy for all cohort students, which includes students hearing from professionals of color within the STEM fields and from STEM department student affairs officers and participating in STEM-related activities such as engineering challenges.

Academic Preparation

The academic preparation component would consist of strengthening the mathematics course offered during the 2-week program as well as adding a STEM course. Although developing a mathematics course that best suits the needs of a diverse learning community has been different in previous years, the future of this component is promising. The mathematics course would focus primarily on building mathematics skills through social justice–oriented project-based learning. The students will work collectively in small groups to address a specific problem facing students of color such as the overrepresentation of Black males in special education, the continued underrepresentation of Black and Latina women in the STEM fields, and the disproportionate number of expulsions of students of color in urban schools. Students would use applied mathematics skills to address particular areas of concern that could include probability and statistics, which requires elements of advanced algebra and calculus. By working in groups with advanced college students, students would be able to share their expertise based on their level of mathematical reasoning as well as learn from their peers. Further, students would have the opportunity to conduct a project using applied mathematics that is relevant to their schooling experiences.

The STEM course would primarily function to increase students' competencies in inquiry-based learning as opposed to a specific content area (e.g., biology, chemistry, physics). This course would be similar to the mathematics class, which currently focuses on a wide variety of mathematical concepts to serve the various needs of students at different levels. In the STEM course, students would complete a short inquiry project each time they meet based on either science, technology, or engineering. Mathematics would be embedded within each of these areas, since there is a separate course for this area. The overall purpose of this component is to potentially increase and sustain student interest in STEM-related fields and build inquiry skills. The ASO would be responsible for recruiting talented educators to teach these courses as well as one undergraduate teaching assistant who would attend each class and work closely with the instructors and students throughout the course.

Undergraduate Persistence

The final component of the ASO's responsibilities would consist of offering effective support for our undergraduate students with STEM-related majors. The ASO would identify the students who are majoring in STEM-related majors during their first quarter on campus and host a welcome session within the first 2 weeks of school. In this session, 1st-year students would mingle with upper-class students in the program pursuing STEM majors, in an effort to build a community within this group. Students would also receive information regarding academic support available to them by the university such as peer learning. The ASO would also serve as a liaison between the program and the STEM departments on campus by reaching out to the student affairs officers within each department. Through this partnership, the ASO would be responsible for keeping abreast of opportunities for academic support and joining academic and career-related organizations, undergraduate research opportunities, and programs focused on preparing students for STEM-related careers. In addition to receiving this support from the ASO, students in the program would be encouraged to work together in an effort to offer peer support through academic tutoring, study sessions, or group accountability.

Collectively, these initiatives provide an opportunity to strengthen our program to ensure that students are provided with the support necessary to achieve their academic goal of successfully completing STEM degrees. It is without question that the scholars stand to benefit exponentially from program expansion as we learn more about the needs of our students beyond our initial focus from when the program was developed a decade ago. The following section examines a significant area of concern related to our ability to sustain the success we have experienced thus far: recruiting eligible students. More specifically, the program would like to recruit more eligible Black males, especially from schools in the program that have historically struggled to provide sufficient Black males within their applicant pool. Without a diverse applicant pool in terms of gender, the program stands to serve a disproportionate number of female students from certain schools, which does little to address concerns for increasing the number of Black males attending postsecondary institutions nationwide.

EARLY OUTREACH:
INCREASING PROGRAM ELIGIBILITY OF BLACK MALES

One significant goal of the program is to recruit cohorts with greater gender balance, as there are often challenges recruiting males, more specifically Black males, into the program each year. Educational research and outreach concerning Black males has grown significantly to address their schooling experiences and academic outcomes (Howard, 2008; Howard, Flennaugh, & Terry, 2012; Jordan & Cooper, 2003; Noguera, 2003). The program has recruited a number of Black males who have gone on to experience great academic success. However, it is imperative that we are better able to serve more Black males and to combat challenges they face within their schools that thwart their college admittance rates.

Jordan and Cooper (2003) point out the shortcomings of school reform efforts in adequately addressing educational issues concerning Black males. The authors argue, "The strategies often used in high school reform represent a responsible but incomplete approach to addressing the needs of Black male adolescents" (p. 213). Considering the damaging schooling experiences they face in the United States largely because of a history of negative social and academic presuppositions regarding Black maleness (Howard, 2008, 2014; Howard, Flennaugh, & Terry, 2012; Noguera, 2003), it is vital that research and reform efforts further consider the role of mentorship among Black males. In addition, it is especially important to consider those who demonstrate cultural congruence with Black males, which may serve as a significant asset for effective mentorship (Jordan & Cooper, 2003).

As outlined in the program description in Chapter 2, scholars are recruited during their sophomore year of high school. Unfortunately, the program has encountered difficulty recruiting eligible Black males because of challenges many encounter during their freshman year. More specifically, recruitment has been a challenge at select schools because of low grade point averages among 10th-graders, especially Black males. The program traditionally contacts students midway through their sophomore year; however, the students have already completed three semesters in high school without direct guidance from the program's mentors. To address this concern, some mentors have begun outreaching to 9th-grade students to encourage them to work toward earning higher grade point averages in an effort to increase the eligible applicant pool. While this outreach has garnered noticeable improvement in recruitment from select schools, we believe a more directed effort must ensue to yield the outcomes the program desires.

Program stakeholders foresee developing a more structured feature of the program to increase the number of competitive Black male applicants that will become an integral phase of VIP Scholars, such as developing a summer program specifically for Black male youth. Within the cohorts of underrepresented students of color, the number of eligible Black male applicants remains scarce; thus a pipeline program is essential, for several reasons. A significant number of students are susceptible to going down an academic track that does not lead to postsecondary matriculation as early as the first semester of their 9th-grade year. We seek to begin structured mentorship during their first year as well as offer a summer program for Black males. The primary focus of this early outreach aspect of the program is to prepare students for the rigor of the college preparatory track early on and offer guidance to maintain satisfactory grade point averages. Targeting Black males with a host of workshops and a strong mentorship component will undoubtedly create a larger pool of Black male applicants and subsequently increase their representation in the tradition summer cohorts.

Summer Program

In attempt to respond to the dearth of Black males, the program hopes to begin with a cohort of 50 students, all 9th-grade Black males, from five surrounding schools that serve a large number of Black students. These 50 students would participate in their own 6-week summer program directly before their sophomore year. We hope to recruit at least 10 students from each school, and special consideration would be given to students who participate in the free and reduced-price lunch program. These students would be mentored by undergraduate Black males attending UCLA who have demonstrated a commitment to the educational outcomes of Black males through assisting with educational research. The primary goal of these mentors is to serve as quasi–college counselors for participants and promote a college-going culture within selected schools. This early step is essential to address any academic shortcomings that the young men have early in their high school careers, and to increase their college knowledge as they start high school. Each participant would have up to two assigned mentors whose responsibility would be to ensure that the youth are aware of the postsecondary educational opportunities available to them. In addition, the mentors would help the participants gain a better understanding of the college application process, as many students are left without guidance when they apply to college. Mentors also keep in contact with their mentees' teachers and their course curriculum, which will aid mentors in effectively advocating on their mentees' behalf. Further, mentors would also serve as tutors for their mentees and would facilitate workshops for the participants.

Similar to the guidance offered to cohort students, the mentors would dedicate 12 hours each to their students during the summer program, which would consist of at least 4 hours of individual meetings to discuss their academic, social, and emotional well-being. The remaining time is spent offering small- and whole-group sessions that alternate throughout the week and during the weekend. Part of this work would also include working with the parents, guardians, or caregivers of the young men to help inform them about the college going process as well.

Postsecondary Preparation

The mentors for the young men would help students become better acclimated to the campus through tours, which would serve as a way to make participants genuinely excited about attending an institution of higher learning. Students would also attend workshops that would provide them with information on different universities and offer and describe ways to become a more competitive applicant through completing advanced coursework and participating in extracurricular activities. Students would also receive academic tutoring within areas of concern that will help them gain study tips and receive ACT and SAT preparation assistance through professional service providers on weekends throughout the academic year. Additional support focused on improving the students' reading comprehension and writing skills would also be offered. Here, the mentors would emphasize the tools that students can use in the future to prepare for essays in Advanced Placement courses and college application essays. Finally, each student would complete a 4-year plan with assistance from his mentor to ensure that he is on track to completing the course requirements for admittance into 4-year universities.

LOCAL, STATE, AND FEDERAL RECOMMENDATIONS

This final section of this chapter offers recommendations for local, statewide, and national stakeholders with a vested interest in activating sustainable change in college access for low-income students of color. The VIPS program is an excellent example of how one program can garner support from multiple stakeholders through partnerships between the school districts served, VIPS schools, UCLA, private donors, and individual supporters. Each group of stakeholders serves different purposes for the overall function of the program, which aids in meeting the overall goal of providing access to postsecondary opportunities for our scholars. The recommendations below focus primarily on three levels of support: local, state, and national. Given the link between community stakeholders and the program, discussed at length in a previous section, the following will highlight how we can move forward in terms of programmatic thrusts, policy, and research within these three levels of support.

Local Recommendations

As previously described, the VIPS program is located in Los Angeles and serves schools in both the Los Angeles Unified School District and the Pasadena Unified District. This university partnership between the schools and UCLA not only aids in building a stronger college going culture within these schools but also provides an additional avenue to carry out the university's mission and values. On a local level, it is essential that schools are intentional and relentless in their efforts to build a strong college-going culture that garners results. Doing so requires policies and programmatic efforts at the district and schoolwide levels that require stronger relationships with local universities (Miller & Hafner, 2008).

The Center for Higher Education Policy Analysis denoted five essential elements of building college-going culture through their analyses of research on college access and college culture within schools (Corwin & Tierney, 2007). The authors identify the following as essential to building this culture: academic momentum, an understanding of how college plans develop, a clear mission statement, comprehensive college services, and coordinated and systemic college support. Programs such as VIPS assist with offering the comprehensive services and college support high schools need to build this culture. With very few college counselors at schools nationwide to adequately provide the comprehensive services necessary to ensure that all students are assisted in their college choice process, university-sponsored programs are vital. In many instances, university-sponsored programs may be all that students have where college preparation is concerned. Beyond the counselor shortage, McDonough

(2005a) shares that some counselors describe college counseling as "esoteric" and outside their role as "mental health agents" (p. 10).

Considering this, schools must ensure that counselors are trained each year with updated information about the university admissions processes, especially at highly selective institutions with varied admissions requirements. For example, the admissions requirements for the University of California and the California State University schools vary significantly. It is imperative that counselors are updated about any changes in required coursework for admissions, especially for those scholars creating 4-year plans within their freshman year. Developing ongoing partnerships with institutions will thwart chances that scholars are making course decisions based on outdated information provided by their schools. Further, building strong relationships with universities through college outreach programs may also provide opportunities to expand the shared responsibility between universities and schools to provide college access opportunities. Although there is a shortage of counselors, college outreach programs should serve to *enhance* the college choice process as opposed to essentially taking the place of adequate counseling that should be provided to all students.

In addition to relationships between school districts and universities being built, it is vital that districts directly address issues concerning college access, especially those schools that serve a majority of low-income students of color. By referencing the practices of successful programs such as VIPS, districts have the opportunity to create avenues for their students to become college bound that are beyond the traditional methods focused solely on high school graduation or on meeting "college readiness" standards. While focusing on students becoming "college ready" from a curriculum standpoint, this focus alone has done very little to close the access gap and may have widened it through limited access to Advanced Placement courses in schools that serve primarily students of color (Teranishi et al., 2004). Districts must move beyond evaluating schools based on test scores and adequate yearly progress per the requirements of the No Child Left Behind Act and consider whether schools are meeting students' goals of entering college upon graduating from high school. Should districts and the schools within them continue to turn a blind eye to an overwhelming number of their low-income students of color enrolling primarily in community colleges and for-profit institutions, or in no colleges at all, they will continue to ultimately fail the very people they were created to serve.

Statewide Recommendations

There are three primary recommendations for consideration at the state level: engage in program evaluation of college outreach programs, reexamine the role of community colleges as it relates to 4-year college access, and expand training and credentialing for college counseling.

At the higher education level, states should evaluate the effectiveness of college outreach programs within their publicly funded universities to determine whether they are directly addressing college access in a meaningful way. The Educational Policy Institute (Swail, Quinn, Landis, & Fung, 2012) identified common themes across effective college outreach programs that include intentionality, focus on students and student/parent efficacy, data-driven practices, program management, intrusiveness, high expectations, and sustainability. Our program expands on commonly accepted practices by incorporating a focus on social justice. As a starting point, states should consider which factors are essential for their state-funded outreach programs and designate a baseline set of criteria to determine a program's effectiveness. Although programs should have the autonomy to set their own missions and means of meeting program goals, a baseline set of objectives may be more effective in adequately determining which programs are meeting the overall goal of increasing college access opportunities.

Although our program focuses solely on preparing scholars for matriculation into selective 4-year universities, we must not forget that many students of color enroll in community colleges after graduation and for varied reasons. Those students with the intent to continue to 4-year universities should be provided with similar guidance in the admissions process as that of those students who chose to go directly into a 4-year program; thus community college must create better "transfer-going cultures" (Handel, 2007, p. 44). In addition, like college counselors at the high school level, those advising students at the community college level should be kept abreast of changes in admissions requirements and, most important, the articulation agreements between their institutions and others (Handel, 2007). In addition, students with the intent to transfer to selective universities should be aware of the transfer rates and articulation agreements between certain community colleges before they choose to enroll, which Handel (2007) suggests can be shared within a "transfer centers" developed on community college campuses (p. 45).

Keeping this in mind, it also important that states evaluate the transfer rates between their community colleges and 4-year universities to determine potential differences based on the racial composition of the community college. Just as scholars determined that racial composition has an impact on college matriculation at the high school level (Teranishi et al., 2004), similar findings could also exist at the community college level. Finally, more states should take a more proactive approach toward building stronger partnerships between community colleges and 4-year universities beyond articulation agreements on coursework. Considering that students attend community college for various reasons, as opposed to the common belief that one is not ready for "college level" coursework, knowing how to create stronger partnerships is vital (Kisker, 2007). Further, partnerships between community colleges and universities located in the same city demonstrate a stronger commitment to the local area on behalf of the postsecondary institution by addressing the expressed need to increase educational opportunities (Miller & Hafner, 2008). One such program within UCLA, the Center for Community College Programs, is representative of an effective partnership between the university and local community colleges in Los Angeles County.

The final statewide recommendation includes offering degree programs and credentialing for those interested solely in offering college counseling. As noted by McDonough (2005a), school counselors are not in total agreement about the incorporation of college counseling within their roles. This is understandably so when one becomes familiar with the coursework required for school counseling programs, which are often required for school counselor positions. The set of knowledge and skills required of an effective college counselor does not align with the training of a school counselor, who is trained as a mental health professional. Because of this disconnect between different skills sets, it would be essential to create professional programs and credential certificates that are specifically geared toward preparing the college counselor. Together, these recommendations are only a starting point for states to address pathways for postsecondary access for their students.

Federal, Nationwide Approach

There are three main recommendations for a national approach: increase funding for college outreach programs, address the college counselor shortage, and increase research funding for college outreach programs.

First, programs such as VIPS rely heavily or almost exclusively on state funding through their respective universities and private donors. There should be increased opportunities for university programs to receive federal funding to operate. Expanding funding opportunities for programs that are not under the umbrella of the federal TRiO program expands our reach for providing college access to students with different interests and needs. For example, our firm commitment to social justice and developing the next generation of change agents is a component that is not easily found within other programs and may be appealing to students who hope to create social change.

In addition to increasing funding opportunities, it is essential that issues concerning college counselors and their impact on creating strong college-bound cultures are considered. Although explained in the previous section on state recommendations, this issue should not solely rest on the shoulders of the state. The Department of Education should make college counseling a national agenda (McDonough, 2005) if we are to address the concern regarding historically underrepresented scholars' postsecondary enrollment. This is especially important given the focus on increasing STEM college graduates domestically to fill projected STEM-related jobs. Without adequately addressing the gap between those who have access to college counseling and those who do not, this proposed initiative is only a fantasy. On a federal level, grants and scholarships for professionals to pursue emerging college counseling programs could possibly attract more educators with a commitment to do this work.

Finally, providing federal funds to conduct program evaluation research on college outreach programs is vital to programs with limited budgets. By funding more research grants to university college outreach programs such as VIPS, they will be able to more effectively determine successes and areas of growth for their programs. Although substantial funding is allocated to college outreach programs that are federally funded, it is essential that additional grants are made available for those programs that do not rely on federal funds to operate. Doing so demonstrates a commitment on behalf of the federal government to improve external programs in an effort to better serve a wider range of students. These programs can serve only a specific number of students each year and are restricted to conducting the program as outlined by their funding sources. Thus, supplementing external programs with grants solely for the purpose of program evaluation provides the necessary funding to fulfill this need without jeopardizing the integrity of the program through peripheral rules and regulations.

College outreach programs should have access to research funds made available through federal initiatives that seek to address the postsecondary pathways of underrepresented groups in any given area such as My Brother's Keeper and STEM initiatives. It important that these initiatives connect themselves with programs with a sustained history of moving beyond the college access rhetoric by taking action to address this issue head on. Collectively, these recommendations at the local, state, and federal levels are but a starting point in an ongoing battle to increase postsecondary pathways for historically marginalized students.

Eight

Recommendations

Jonli D. Tunstall, Terry K. Flennaugh, and Tyrone C. Howard

RECOMMENDATIONS FOR POLICYMAKERS

The importance of higher education continues to grow. Despite concerns raised about the proposed value of education (Anyon, 2014), what remains evident is the clear and consistent correlation between education and overall quality of life. Data tells us that education brings about greater political participation, better access to health care and longer life expectancy, fewer engagements in substance abuse and criminal activity, and higher lifetime earning (Krueger et al., 2015). In short, education matters. Higher education matters even more when it comes to transforming life chances for historically marginalized groups and underserved communities. The work captured in this book speaks to the important work being done by students, faculty, administrators, and staff as part of the VIP Scholars program. While this work is important, it represents only a small fraction of what needs to be done nationally around college access for underrepresented groups. To that end, there needs to be larger set of policy implications tied to this topic for larger-scale transformation. In this section we highlight potential policy recommendations that would assist in this topic of college access.

1. Greater Counseling Supports

One of the areas of concern that we heard from students throughout the course of the program is that VIP Scholars provided students with information and resources that their schools did not provide about college and college preparation. Some students lamented that their schools did not have college counselors or had few counselors available to them, or they spoke about the scarcity of counselors in general who placed primary focus on high school graduation and much less on college. An important policy implication would be to ensure that all schools, but especially those with underrepresented populations (and limited resources), have better counselor-to-student ratios. According to the U.S. Department of Education, the American School Counselor Association recommends a student-to-counselor ratio of 250 to 1. In states such as California, the ratio was 1,016 to 1 for the 2010–2011 school year, the latest for which data are available. In many urban districts such as Los Angeles County those numbers are even higher. Not only are school counselors vital in college and career readiness; they also can be helpful in personal and social development. Effective counseling programs are important also to school climate and student achievement. Thus from a policy standpoint, district and state mandates should require that student-to-counselor ratios be in compliance with recommended ratios to ensure students reasonable access to high school counselors who can offer much needed college and career supports that are often lacking in low-income schools and neighborhoods.

2. University Supports

Universities should and must play a pivotal role in increasing access for underserved populations. To that end, state legislators should consider tying various financial supports to university outreach efforts to underserved schools and communities. While a number of federally funded programs are currently in place across the nation (which should continue to be supported and even expanded), we would argue that policymakers should require that universities demonstrate data-driven results of such programs and how they are committed to their overall mission of inclusion and representation of students from underserved backgrounds. Furthermore, important policy ramifications should be required that incentivize university–school partnerships. The greater the degree of transparency for schools around university access, the clearer the pathways become. We would also suggest policy efforts that focus on strengthening school–university partnerships with an explicit focus on improved access to college and career readiness. A growing number of colleges have either formally opened or sanctioned university K–12 schools or have adopted charters and co-govern such institutions. Structured, sustained, and resource-intensive partnerships such as these demonstrate a vested interest on the part of universities to play an instrumental role in K–12 schools that prepare students for college and career readiness.

3. Revisiting Race-Based Admissions

One of the biggest obstacles for greater access to institutions of higher education has been the removal of race as a consideration in admissions. As institutions continue to promote a diversity agenda, a closer look at various universities nationally suggests that many fall short of the mark. As we have documented in this work, a number of states, such as California, Texas, Michigan, and Washington, have statewide bans of race-based considerations for college admissions. We would argue that states reconsider such bans and examine their utility in 2016. As stated earlier in this book, the effects of initiatives such as California's Proposition 209 have led to a direct decrease in the number of African American and Latino students in some of the state's most prestigious universities. As issues surrounding the *Fisher* case continue to examine the role of race in university admissions, we strongly advise that states with affirmative action bans reintroduce the debate, consider the effects of such policies, and rethink or identify creative legislation and policies that take into consideration social, political, historical, and educational obstacles faced by many students of color. What we would call for are policies that pay particular attention to race in admissions. The College Board (2008) draws a distinct line between race-conscious policies and race-neutral ones where college admission is concerned. They state:

> Race-conscious policies include two types of policies: (1) those that involve explicit racial classifications (such as the University of Michigan Law School's race-as-a-factor admissions policy, where race was an express factor used in evaluating applicants); and (2) those that are neutral on their face but that are motivated by a racially discriminatory purpose, resulting in racially discriminatory effects. Thus, facially neutral policies may in some cases actually qualify as race-conscious, given the underlying motivation. (The question that the U.S. Supreme Court has not definitively addressed in a higher education enrollment management setting is "how much" of a racially discriminatory motivation is necessary in order for such policies to qualify as race-conscious.)
>
> Race-neutral policies include two types of policies: (1) those that, with respect to both operation (read: language) and intent, are neutral; and (2) those "inclusive" outreach and recruitment policies that expand efforts to generate additional applicant interest, which may be facially race-conscious and/or race conscious in intent, but which do not confer material benefits to the exclusion of non-targeted students.

RECOMMENDATIONS FOR K-12 SCHOOLS

This work provides a program model addressing college access, educational pipelines, and critical consciousness among historically marginalized and underserved students of color. Understanding and examining the impact of a social justice college access program on students, families, and communities has powerful implications for educators, partnerships, and all those interested in increasing college access for underrepresented students. One major barrier affecting the enrollment rates and level of preparation of African American and other underrepresented students at selective institutions is the lack of communication and connection between the K–12 and higher education systems (Kirst & Bracco, 2004). This is evident in the lack of clear dissemination of information, the misaligned curricula, and a culture of low expectations that exists across the system (Kirst & Bracco, 2004). We argue that in order to increase opportunities for all students to gain access to, prepare for, attend, and graduate from postsecondary institutions, there must be better alignment and communication across the K–16 system.

1. Cultivating Stronger K-16 Partnerships

The work in this book demonstrates a robust university–community–school partnership and its impact on individual students, families, and the university. In effective partnerships, all partners involved work in collaboration to coordinate and implement programs and activities aimed at increasing the academic, emotional, and social success of students served by the school (Davies, 1996; Epstein, 1995). Effective communication across the K–16 system includes the free flow of information back and forth, providing students, teachers, parents, and counselors with college knowledge (Kirst & Bracco, 2004). Because of the overcrowding of schools and classrooms, high schools often do not have any or enough counselors who focus solely on providing information on college. With a high student-to-counselor ratio at the high school level, few counselors are able to spend a substantial amount of time on postsecondary issues (Venezia & Kirst, 2005). This displays an even greater need for a better-integrated K–16 system. Further, while strides have been made, there is still a need for better alignment of high school graduation requirements and college acceptance requirements. This could also include providing additional time for more professional development opportunities for counselors and teachers to become better aware of changes and updates in college admissions requirements. This serves to improve students' college knowledge within the schools and decreases the sole reliance on college outreach programs to provide this.

Establishing effective partnerships with colleges and universities not only increases individual student success; research indicates that school–family–community partnerships improve school programs and school climate, as well as increase parent and family engagement in the school and community (Epstein, 1995; Henderson & Mapp, 2002). The benefits of strong partnerships between universities and high schools are far reaching and have a ripple effect on the schools, homes, and communities in which the students reside.

2. Validating Students' Culture Within the School

Although school–family–community partnerships are not a panacea for addressing issues of access and equity that students from urban schools encounter, they foster protective factors that help students overcome some of the barriers and risks that many students from urban schools and communities encounter (Bryan, 2005). Recognizing and addressing these barriers must take place not only within programs but also within the school. This acknowledges the imperative of creating spaces within and outside the classroom that validate students' background and culture. This cannot just happen during Black History Month or cultural holidays but must take place throughout the year and encompass more than an assembly. Students of color attending urban schools often feel powerless in a majority-dominated school culture where language, class, and culture differences are seen as deficits (Cummins, 1986; Noguera, 1996, 2001). Providing safe spaces and culturally relevant curricula increases student engagement and enables students to connect their lived experiences with their academic experiences. This situates schools as a place that cultivates both high achievers and cultural pride. This is imperative for K–12 school leaders who are invested in creating sustainable, social justice–oriented learning experiences for students as they prepare for higher education.

RECOMMENDATIONS FOR INSTITUTIONS OF HIGHER EDUCATION

Colleges and universities (especially land-grant institutions) have an obligation to increase the pool of those students who are included in the applicant pool and subsequently admitted and who come from underserved and systemically marginalized communities. While previous chapters have outlined a number of action items that colleges and universities can follow to be more genuine in their efforts to build meaningful partnerships with communities traditionally underrepresented and underserved on their campuses, it is worth reiterating two specific ideas here based on the work of the VIP Scholars program.

1. Laying Out a Bold Vision for Inclusion

College and university administrators across the country are finding it increasingly difficult to not be confronted with the fact that students on their campuses (particularly students of color) are fed up with instances of casual, everyday racism (Binkley & Whack, 2015). As opposed to putting their proverbial heads in the sand, administrators at institutions of higher education must recognize that these incidences are symptomatic of broader societal structures that place more value on the experiences and lives of White people than on the experiences and lives of people of color. Rather than sitting idly by while students struggle with notions of privilege and oppression in spaces ill equipped to foster opportunities for meaningful dialogue and learning, university and college leaders must lay out a bold vision for diversity and inclusion on their campuses that is informed by notions of equity and social justice. Some potential components of a plan might include the appointment of a diversity and inclusion administrator (with appropriate institutional support and power), the creation of a diversity curriculum that would be a requirement for undergraduate students, mandated diversity training for faculty and staff, the creation of a multicultural student center, the creation of ethnic studies departments, and prioritizing the hiring of faculty and staff from underrepresented communities. These are only a few recommendations that colleges and universities can enact, but an important component in any effort to address diversity and inclusion on a campus must include the time-consuming work of building consensus among campus partners such as students. Any effort initiated without the input of students and other campus partners will not likely solicit the needed buy-in to make initiatives successful.

2. Establishing Genuine Relationships with Pre-K–12 Schools

The previous section laid out the imperative of a stronger alignment across the K–16 system. A vital question for university and college administrators to ask themselves is whether their engagement with surrounding communities connects university knowledge with community knowledge in mutually beneficial ways. An unfortunate reality for far too many communities near institutions of higher education is that the nature of the relationship disproportionally benefits colleges and universities that use communities as sites for research and for enriching the experiences of undergraduate students who themselves are not from the community. Faculty research, field placements, and community service activities devoid of meaningful efforts to shift how the university operates in response to needs voiced by the community only perpetuate the paternalistic relationships that many institutions of higher education have with surrounding communities and their schools. This stance furthers deficit-oriented views about the perceived wealth in certain communities and the value of developing mutually beneficial relationships with certain communities. The nature of this relationship has not been lost on community schools that are understandably hesitant in granting access to university-affiliated programs. Nonetheless, it is vitally important that university and college administrators begin the process of building trust with community schools by providing students from these communities with the necessary tools and resources to pursue admission to, enroll in, and graduate from their institution. Developing pipeline programs in partnership with communities is perhaps one of the most effective ways to develop responsible and genuine relationships with communities that disrupt both the absence and one-sided "exchanges" that have become far too representative of the presence of universities in their surrounding communities.

References

Ahn, J. (2010). The role of social network locations in the college access mentoring of urban youth. *Education and Urban Society, 42*(7), 839–859.

Alexander, M. (2010). *The new Jim Crow: Mass incarceration in the age of colorblindness.* New York, NY: The New Press.

Allen, W. R. (1988). Black students in US higher education: Toward improved access, adjustment, and achievement. *The Urban Review, 20*(3), 165–188.

Allen, W. R., & Solorzano, D. G. (2001). Affirmative action, educational equity, and campus racial climate: A case study of the University of Michigan Law School. *Berkeley La Raza Law Journal, 12,* 237–263.

Anderson, J. A. (1988). *The education of Blacks in the South, 1860–1935.* Chapel Hill, NC: University of North Carolina Press.

Anyon, J. (1980). Social class and the hidden curriculum of work. *Journal of Education, 67*–92.

Anyon, J. (2014). *Radical possibilities: Public policy, urban education, and a new social movement,* (2nd ed.). New York, NY: Routledge.

Astin, A. W. (1975). *Preventing students from dropping out.* San Francisco, CA: Jossey-Bass.

Astin, A. W. (1987). Retaining and satisfying students. *Educational Record, 68*(1), 36–42.

Astin, A. W. (1993). *What matters in college? Four critical years revisited.* San Francisco, CA: Jossey-Bass.

Aud, S., Fox, M., & KewalRamani, A. (2010). *Status and trends in the education of racial and ethnic groups* (NCES 2010-015). U.S. Department of Education, National Center for Education Statistics. Washington, DC: U.S. Government Printing Office.

Aud, S., Hussar, W., Johnson, F., Kena, G., Roth, E., Manning, E., Wang, X., & Zhang, J. (2012). *The condition of education 2012* (NCES 2012-045). U.S. Department of Education, National Center for Education Statistics. Washington, DC. Available at http://nces.ed.gov/pubsearch

Aud, S., Wilkinson-Flicker, S., Kristapovich, P., Rathbun, A., Wang, X., & Zhang, J. (2013). *The condition of education 2013* (NCES 2013-037). U.S. Department of Education, National Center for Education Statistics. Washington, DC: Government Printing Office.

Auerbach, S. (2007). From moral supporters to struggling advocates: Reconceptual-izing parent roles in education through the experience of working-class families of color. *Urban Education, 42*(3), 250–283.

Avery, C., & Kane, T. J. (2004). Student perceptions of college opportunities: The Boston coach program. In C. M. Hoxby (Ed.), *College choices: The economics of where to go, when to go, and how to pay for it* (pp. 355–394). Chicago, IL: University of Chicago Press.

Bandura, A. (1977). Self-efficacy: Toward a unifying theory of behavioral change. *Psychological Review, 84*(2), 191–215.

Bandura, A. (1997). *Self-efficacy: The exercise of control.* New York, NY: W. H. Free-man.

Banks, J. A. (2015). *Cultural diversity and education: Foundations, curriculum, and teaching* (6th ed.). New York, NY: Pearson.

Baum, S., Ma, J., & Payea, K. (2013). *Education pays 2013: The benefits of higher ed-ucation for individuals and society.* Washington, DC: College Board. Available at trends.collegeboard.org/sites/default/files/education-pays-2013-full-report.pdf

Bell, D. A. (1995). Who's afraid of critical race theory? *University of Illinois Law Review,* (4), 893–910.

Benson, P. L., & Scales, P. C. (2009). Positive youth development and the prevention of youth aggression and violence. *International Journal of Developmental Science, 3*(3), 218–234.

Binkley, C., & Whack, E. H. (2015, November 12). In the wake of Missouri uproar, Black students around U.S. complain of casual, everyday racism. *U.S. News and World Report.* Available at www.usnews.com/news/us/articles/2015/11/12/mis-souri-protests-embolden-student-leaders-on-other-campuses

Blackwell, J. E. (1989). Mentoring: An action strategy for increasing minority facul-ty. *Academe, 75*(5), 8–14. Available at www.jstor.org.proxy2.library.illinois.edu/stable/40249734

Bonilla-Silva, E. (2011, April 6–8). *The real race problem in sociology: The power of White rule in our discipline.* Presidential plenary address, presented at the South-ern Sociological Society meeting, Jacksonville, FL.

Bourdieu, P. (1977). *Outline of a theory of practice* (Vol. 16). Oxford, UK: Cambridge University Press.

Bourdieu, P. (1986). The forms of capital. In J. G. Richardson (Ed.), *Handbook of theory and research for the sociology of education,* (pp. 241–258). New York, NY: Greenwood.

Brewer, E. W., & Landers, J. M. (2005). A longitudinal study of the talent search program. *Journal of Career Development, 31*(3), 195–208.

Bruce, M., & Bridgeland, J. (2014). *The mentoring effect: Young people's perspectives on the outcomes and availability of mentoring.* Washington, DC: Civic Enterprises with Hart Research Associates for MENTOR: The National Mentoring Partner-ship. Available at http://www.civicenterprises.net/Education

Bryan, J. (2005). Fostering educational resilience and achievement in urban schools through school-family-community partnerships. *Professional School Counseling, 8,* 219–227.

Burris, C. C., Wiley, E. W., Welner, K. G., & Murphy, J. (2008). Accountability, rigor, and detracking: Achievement effects of embracing a challenging curriculum as a universal good for all students. *Teachers College Record, 110*(3), 571–608.

Cabrera, A. F., & La Nasa, S. M. (2000a). Overcoming the tasks on the path to college for America's disadvantaged. *New Directions for Institutional Research, 2000*(107), 31–43.

Cabrera, A. F., & La Nasa, S. M. (2000b). Understanding the college-choice process. *New Directions for Institutional Research, 2000*(107), 5–22.

Cabrera, A. F., & La Nasa, S. M. (2001). On the path to college: Three critical tasks facing America's disadvantaged. *Research in Higher Education, 42*(2), 119–149.

Cabrera, A. F., Deil-Amen, R., Prabhu, R, Terenzini, P. T., Lee, C., & Franklin, R. (2006). Increasing the college preparedness of at-risk students. *Journal of Latinos and Education, 5,* 79–97.

California State Department of Education. (1960). *A master plan for higher education in California, 1960-1975.* Sacramento, CA: California State Department of Education. Available at http://www.ucop.edu/acadinit/mastplan/MasterPlan1960.pdf

Callan, P. M. (2009). Reframing access and opportunity: Public policy dimensions. In D. E. Heller (Ed.), *The states and public higher education policy: Affordability, access, and accountability,* (pp. 87–105). Baltimore, MD: The Johns Hopkins University Press.

Campaign for College Opportunity. (2015). *Access denied: Rising selectivity at California's public universities.* Sacramento, CA. Available at http://collegecampaign.org/wp-content/uploads/2015/05/2015-Access-Denied_Full-Report_FINAL.pdf.

Carnevale, A., Rose, S., & Cheah, B. (2011). *The college payoff: Education, occupations, lifetime earnings.* Washington, DC: Georgetown University Center on Education and the Workforce. Available at cew.georgetown.edu/wp-content/uploads/2014/11/collegepayoff-complete.pdf

Carnevale, A., & Strohl, J. (2013). *Separate and unequal: How higher education reinforces the intergenerational reproduction of White racial privilege.* Washington, DC: Georgetown University Center on Education and the Workforce. Available at www9.georgetown.edu/grad/gppi/hpi/cew/pdfs/Separate&Unequal.FR.pdf

Carter, D. J. (2008). Achievement as resistance: The development of a critical race achievement ideology among Black achievers. *Harvard Educational Review, 78*(3), 466–497.

Carter, P. L., & Wellner, K. G. (2013). *Closing the opportunity gap: What America must do to give every child an even chance.* Oxford, UK: Oxford University Press.

Cass, J. (2010). *Held captive: Child poverty in America.* Washington, DC: Children's Defense Fund. Available at www.cdfohio.org/research-library/documents/resources/poverty_report_2010_finalpdf.pdf

Center on Society and Health. (2014). *Education: It matters more to health than ever before*. Richmond, VA: Virginia Commonwealth University Center on Society and Health. Available at www.rwjf.org/content/dam/farm/reports/issue_briefs/2014/rwjf409883

Children's Defense Fund. (2014). *Child poverty in America 2013*: National analysis. Available at www.childrensdefense.org/zzz-child-research-data-publications/data/child-poverty-in-america-2013.pdf

Cohen, G. L., & Prinstein, M. J. (2006). Peer contagion of aggression and health-risk behavior among adolescent males: An experimental investigation of effects on public conduct and private attitudes. *Child Development, 77*(4), 967–983.

Cohen, G. L., Steele, C. M., & Ross, L. D. (1999). The mentor's dilemma: Providing critical feedback across the racial divide. *Personality and Social Psychology Bulletin, 25*(10), 1302–1318.

Coleman, J. S., Campbell, E. Q., Hobson, C. J., McPartland, J., Mood, A. M., Weinfeld, F. D., & York, R. (1966). *Equality of educational opportunity*. Washington, DC: U.S. Government Printing Office.

Collaborative for Academic, Social, and Emotional Learning. (2014). *What is social emotional learning?* Available at www.casel.org/social-and-emotional-learning/

College Board. (2008). *Race-neutral policies in higher education: From theory to action. A policy paper prepared in conjunction with the College Board's access & diversity collaborative*. New York, NY: Author.

College Board. (2012). *The 8th annual AP report to the nation*. New York, NY: Author. Available at media.collegeboard.com/digitalServices/public/pdf/ap/rtn/AP-Report-to-the-Nation.pdf

Cooper, C. R., Jackson, J. F., Azmitia, M., Lopez, E., & Dunbar, N. (1995). Bridging students' multiple worlds: African American and Latino youth in academic outreach programs. In R. F. Macias & R. G. Garcia-Ramos (Eds.), *Changing schools for changing students: An anthology of research on language minorities* (pp. 1–15). Santa Barbara, CA: University of California Linguistic Minority Research Institute.

Corwin, Z. B., & Tierney, W. G. (2007). *Getting there—and beyond: Building a culture of college going in high schools*. Los Angeles, CA: USC Center for Higher Education Policy Analysis.

Crenshaw, K., Gotanda, N., Peller, G., & Thomas, K. (Eds.). (2000). *Critical race theory: The key writings that formed the movement*. New York, NY: The New Press.

Crisp, G., & Cruz, I. (2009). Mentoring college students: A critical review of the literature between 1990 and 2007. *Research in Higher Education, 50*, 525–545. doi:10.1007/s11162-009-9130-2/

Cummins, J. (1986). Empowering minority students: A framework for intervention. *Harvard Educational Review, 56*(1), 18–37.

Daloz, L. A. (1999). *Mentor: Guiding the journey of adult learners*. San Francisco, CA: Jossey-Bass.

Darling Hammond, L. (2010). *The flat world and education: How America's commitment to equity will determine our future*. New York, NY: Teachers College Press.

Davidson, M., & Foster-Johnson, L. (2001). Mentoring in the preparation of graduate students of color. *Review of Educational Research, 71*(4), 549–574.

Davies, D. (1996). Partnerships for student success. *New Schools, New Communities, 12*(3), 14–21.

Delgado, R., & Stefancic, J. (2001). *Critical race theory: An introduction*. New York, NY: New York University Press.

Delpit, L. (2006). *Other people's children: Cultural conflict in the classroom*. New York, NY: The New Press.

Delpit, L. (2008). *The skin that we speak: Thoughts on language and culture in the classroom*. New York, NY: The New Press.

Delpit, L. (2013). *"Multiplication is for White people": Raising expectations for other people's children*. New York, NY: The New Press.

Dishion, T. J., Poulin, F., & Burraston, B. (2001). Peer group dynamics associated with iatrogenic effects in group interventions with high-risk young adolescents. In C. Erdley & D. W. Nangle (Eds.), *Damon's new directions in child development: The role of friendship in psychological adjustment* (pp. 79–92). San Francisco, CA: Jossey-Bass.

Domina, T. (2009). What works in college outreach: Assessing targeted and school-wide interventions for disadvantaged students. *Educational Evaluation and Policy Analysis, 31*(2), 127–152.

DuBois, D. L., & Karcher, M. J. (2005). Youth mentoring in contemporary perspective. In D. L. DuBois & M. J. Kracher (Eds.), *Handbook of youth mentoring* (pp. 2–11). Thousand Oaks, CA: Sage Publishing.

DuBois, D. L., Neville, H. A., Parra, G. R., & Pugh-Lilly, A. O. (2002). Testing a new model of mentoring. In G. G. Noam (Ed. in chief) & J. E. Rhodes (Ed.), *A critical view of youth mentoring* (pp. 21–57). San Francisco, CA: Jossey-Bass.

DuBois, D. L., Portillo, N., Rhodes, J. E., Silverthorn, N., & Valentine, J. D. (2011). How effective are mentoring programs for youth? A systematic assessment of the evidence. *Psychological Science in the Public Interest, 12*(2), 7–91.

Duncan-Andrade, J. M. (2005). Developing social justice educators. *Educational Leadership, 62*(6), 70–73.

Duncan-Andrade, J. M. R., & Morrell, E. (2008). *The art of critical pedagogy: Possibilities for moving from theory to practice in urban schools* (Vol. 285). New York, NY: Peter Lang.

Early Assessment Program. (n.d.). *In the California State University*. Available at http://www.calstate.edu/eap/

Education Trust. (2012). *Replenishing opportunity in America: The 2012 midterm report of public higher education systems in the access to success initiative*. Washington, DC: Education Trust. Available at 1k9gl1yevnfp2lpq1dhrqe17.wpengine.

netdna-cdn.com/wp-content/uploads/2013/10/Replenishing_Opportunity_2. pdf

Education Trust. (2013). *Doing away with debt: Using existing resources to ensure college affordability for low and middle-income families.* Washington, DC: Author. Available at 1k9gl1yevnfp2lpq1dhrqe17.wpengine.netdna-cdn.com/wp-content/uploads/2013/10/Doing_Away_With_Debt.pdf

Ekono, M., Yang, J., & Smith, S. (2016). *Young children in deep poverty.* New York, NY: National Center for Children in Poverty, Mailman School of Public Health, Columbia University.

Epstein, J. (1995, May). School/family/community partnerships: Caring for the children we share. *Phi Delta Kappan,* 701–712.

Epstein, J. L., & Dauber, S. L. (1991). School programs and teacher practices of parent involvement in inner-city elementary and middle schools. *The Elementary School Journal, 91*(3), 289–305.

Erickson, F. (2012). Culture and education. In J. Banks (Ed.), *Encyclopedia of diversity in education* (pp. 560–569). Thousand Oaks, CA: Sage.

Fan, X., & Chen, M. (2001). Parental involvement and students' academic achievement: A meta-analysis. *Educational Psychology Review, 13*(1), 1–22.

Farmer-Hinton, R. L., & Adams, T. L. (2006). Social capital and college preparation: Exploring the role of counselors in a college prep school for Black students. *Negro Educational Review, 57*(1/2), 101.

Ford, D. (2013). *Recruiting and retaining culturally different students in gifted education.* Austin, TX: Prufrock Press.

Fordham, S., & Ogbu, J. U. (1986). Black students' school success: Coping with the "burden of 'acting white.'" *The Urban Review, 18*(3), 176–206.

Frantz, C. M., Cuddy, A. J. C., Burnett, M., Ray, H., & Hart, A. (2004). A threat in the computer: The race implicit association test as a stereotype threat experience. *Personality and Social Psychology Bulletin, 30*(12),1611–1624.

Freire, P. (1970). Cultural action for freedom. *Harvard Educational Review, 68*(4), 471–521.

Freire, P. (1972). *Conscientizing as a way of liberating.* Washington, DC: LADOC II.

Freire, P. (1993). *Pedagogy of the oppressed.* New York, NY: Continuum. (Original work published 1970)

Freire, P. (1998). *Pedagogy of freedom: Ethics, democracy, and civic courage.* Lanham, MD: Rowman & Littlefield.

Frey, S. (2013). *Report: College achievement gap persists between African American, white students.* Available at edsource.org/2013/report-college-achievement-gap-between-african-american-and-white-students-persists/53649#.VBe-5-c62zh

Gándara, P. (2002). A study of High School Puente: What we have learned about preparing Latino youth for postsecondary education. *Educational Policy, 16*(4), 474–495.

Gándara, P. C. (1995). *Over the ivy walls: The educational mobility of low-income Chicanos.* New York, NY: SUNY Press.

Gándara, P. C. (2012). From González to Flores: A return to the Mexican room? In O. Santa Ana & C. Bustamante (Eds.), *Arizona firestorm* (pp. 121–144). Lanham, MD: Roman & Littlefield.

Gándara, P., & Bial, D. (2001). *Paving the way to higher education: K–12 interventions for underrepresented students.* Washington, DC: National Center for Education Statistics.

Gay, G., & Abrahams, R. D. (1974). Does the pot melt, boil, or brew? Black children and White assessment procedures. *Journal of School Psychology, 11*(4), 330–340.

Geiser, S., & Santelices, V. (2004). *The role of advanced placement and honors courses in college admissions* (No. CSHE.4.04). Research and Occasional Paper Series. University of California, Berkeley, Center for Studies in Higher Education. Available at cshe.berkeley.edu/publications/docs/ROP.Geiser.4.04.pdf

Ginwright, S., & Cammarota, J. (2002). New terrain in youth development: The promise of a social justice approach. *Social Justice, 29*(4), 82–95.

Ginwright, S., & James, T. (2002). From assets to agents of change: Social justice, organizing, and youth development. *New Directions for Youth Development, 2002*(96), 27–46.

Giroux, H. A. (1988). *Teachers as intellectuals: Toward a critical pedagogy of learning.* Westport, CT: Greenwood.

Giroux, H. (2007, Fall) Educated Hope in Dark Times: Critical Pedagogy for Social Justice. *Our Schools/Our Selves, 17*(1), 195–202.

Glennie, E. J., Dalton, B. W., & Knapp, L. G. (2014). The influence of precollege access programs on postsecondary enrollment and persistence. *Educational Policy.* doi 0895904814531647.

Gonzalez, K. P., Stoner, C., & Jovel, J. E. (2003). Examining the role of social capital in access to college for Latinas: Toward a college opportunity framework. *Journal of Hispanic Higher Education, 2*(2), 146–170.

González, N., Moll, L. C., & Amanti, C. (Eds.). (2013). *Funds of knowledge: Theorizing practices in households, communities, and classrooms.* New York, NY: Routledge.

Gorski, P. (2013). *Reaching and teaching students in poverty: Strategies for erasing the opportunity gap.* New York, NY: Teachers College Press.

Green, C. L., Walker, J. M., Hoover-Dempsey, K. V., & Sandler, H. M. (2007). Parents' motivations for involvement in children's education: An empirical test of a theoretical model of parental involvement. *Journal of Educational Psychology, 99*(3), 532–544.

Griffin, K. A. (2012). Access to higher education. In J. A. Banks (Ed.)., *Encyclopedia of diversity in higher education* (Vol. 2, pp. 1054–1058). New York, NY: Sage.

Grolnick, W. S., Benjet, C., Kurowski, C. O., & Apostoleris, N. H. (1997). Predictors of parent involvement in children's schooling. *Journal of Educational Psychology, 89*(3), 538–548.

Grolnick, W. S., & Slowiaczek, M. L. (1994). Parents' involvement in children's schooling: A multidimensional conceptualization and motivational model. *Child Development, 65*(1), 237–252.

Grossman, J. B., & Tierney, J. P. (1998). Does mentoring work? An impact study of the Big Brothers Big Sisters program. *Evaluation Review 22*(3), 402–425.

Gruenewald, D. A. (2003). The best of both worlds: A critical pedagogy of place. *Educational Researcher, 32*(4), 3–12.

Hamilton, S. F., & Hamilton, M. A. (2004). Contexts for mentoring: Adolescent-adult relationships in workplaces and communities. *Handbook of Adolescent Psychology* (3rd. ed.), (Vol. 2, pp. 395–428). New York, NY: Wiley.

Handel, S. J. (2007, September–October). Second chance, not second class: A blueprint for community-college transfer. *Change*, 38–45.

Hara, S. R., & Burke, D. J. (1998). Parent involvement: The key to improved student achievement. *The School Community Journal, 8*(2), 9–19.

Harper, S. R. (2009). Race-conscious student engagement practices and the equitable distribution of enriching educational experiences. *Liberal Education, 95*(4), 38–45. Available at www.aacu.org/liberaleducation/le-fa09/lefa09_Harper.cfm

Harper, S. R. (2012). *Black male student success in higher education: A report from the national Black male college achievement study*. Philadelphia, PA: University of Pennsylvania, Center for the Study of Race and Equity in Education.

Harper, S. R., & Quaye, S. J. (2015). Making engagement equitable for students in U.S. higher education. In S. J. Quaye & S. R. Harper (Eds.), *Student engagement in higher education: Theoretical perspectives and practical approaches for diverse populations*, (pp. 1–14) New York, NY: Routledge.

Harro, B. (2000). The cycle of socialization. In M. Adams, W. J. Blumenfeld, R. Castañeda, H. W. Hackman, M. L. Peters, & X. Zúñiga (Eds.), *Readings for diversity and social justice: An anthology on racism, antisemitism, sexism, heterosexism, ableism and classism* (pp. 15–21). New York, NY: Routledge

Hearn, J. C. (1991). Academic and nonacademic influences on the college destinations of 1980 high school graduates. *Sociology of Education, 64*(3), 158–171.

Henderson, A. T., & Mapp, K. L. (2002). *A new wave of evidence: The impact of school, family, and community connections on student achievement*. Annual Synthesis 2002. National Center for Family and Community Connections with Schools. Austin, TX.

Herndon, M. K., & Hirt, J. B. (2004). Black students and their families: What leads to success in college. *Journal of Black Studies, 34*(4), 489–513.

Herrera, C., Grossmen, J., Kauh, T., & McMaken, J. (2011). Mentoring in schools: An impact study of Big Brothers Big Sisters school based mentoring. *Child Development, 82*(1), 346–381.

Hoover-Dempsey, K. V., & Sandler, H. M. (1997). Why do parents become involved in their children's education? *Review of Educational Research, 67*(1), 3–42.

Hossler, D., & Gallagher, K. S. (1987). Studying student college choice: A three-phase model and the implications for policymakers. *College and University, 62*(3), 207–221.

Hossler, D., & Stage, F. K. (1992). Family and high school experience influences on the postsecondary educational plans of ninth-grade students. *American Educational Research Journal, 29*(2), 425–451.

Howard, T. C. (2003). "A tug of war for our minds": African American high school students' perceptions of their academic identities and college aspirations. *The High School Journal, 87(1)*, 4–17.

Howard, T. C. (2008). Who really cares? The disenfranchisement of African American males in PreK–12 schools: A critical race theory prospective. *Teachers College Record, 110*(5), 954–985.

Howard, T. C. (2010). *Why race and culture matters in schools: Closing the achievement gap in America's classrooms.* New York, NY: Teachers College Press.

Howard, T. C. (2014). *Black male(d): Peril and promise in the education of African American males.* New York, NY: Teachers College Press.

Howard, T. C., & Flennaugh, T. (2011). Research concerns, cautions, and considerations on Black males in a "post-racial" society. *Race Ethnicity and Education, 14*(1), 105–120.

Howard, T. C., Flennaugh, T. K., & Terry, C. L. (2012, Winter–Spring). Black males, social imagery, and the disruption of pathological identities: Implications for research and teaching, *Educational Foundations, 26*(1-2), 85–102.

Howell, J. S., Kurlaender, M., & Grodsky, E. (2010). Postsecondary preparation and remediation: Examining the effect of the early assessment program at California State University. *Journal of Policy Analysis and Management, 29*(4), 726–748.

Hughes, M., & Demo, D. H. (1989). Self-perceptions of Black Americans: Self-esteem and personal efficacy. *American Journal of Sociology, 95*(1), 132–159.

Hurtado, S., Carter, D. F., & Spuler, A. (1996). Latino student transition to college: Assessing difficulties and factors in successful college adjustment. *Research in Higher Education, 37*(2), 135–157.

Iatarola, P., Conger, D., & Long, M. C. (2011). Determinants of high schools' advanced course offerings. *Educational Evaluation and Policy Analysis, 33*(3), 340–359. doi:10.3102/0162373711398124

Ingram, M., Wolfe, R. B., & Lieberman, J. M. (2007). The role of parents in high-achieving schools serving low-income, at-risk populations. *Education and Urban Society, 39*(4), 479–497.

Jarrett, R. L. (1995). Growing up poor: The family experiences of socially mobile youth in low-income African American neighborhoods. *Journal of Adolescent Research, 10*(1), 111–135.

Jarrett, R. L., Sullivan, P. J., & Watkins, N. D. (2005). Developing social capital through participation in organized youth programs: Qualitative insights from three programs. *Journal of Community Psychology, 33*(1), 41–55.

Jayakumar, U. M., Garces, L. M., & Fernandez, F. (2015). *Affirmative action and racial equity: Considering the* Fisher *case to forge the path ahead*. New York, NY: Routledge.

Jeynes, W. H. (2003). The effects of parental involvement on minority children's academic achievement. *Education and Urban Society, 35*(2), 202–218.

Jones, E. R. (1996). Race and the Supreme Court's 1994–95 term. In G. E. Curry (Ed.), *The affirmative action debate* (pp. 326–336). Reading, MA: Addison-Wesley.

Jones, R. (2001). How parents can support learning. *American School Board Journal, 188*(9), 18–22.

Jordan, W. J., & Cooper, R. (2003). High school reform and Black male students: Limits and possibilities of policy and practice. *Urban Education, 38*(2), 196–216.

Karcher, M. J. (2013). Cross-age peer mentoring. In D. DuBois & M. Karcher (Eds.), *Handbook of youth mentoring* (2nd ed., pp. 2–12). Thousand Oaks, CA: Sage.

Keller, T. E. (2005). The stages and development of mentoring relationships. In D. L. DuBois & M. Karcher (Eds.), *Handbook of youth mentoring* (pp. 82–99). Thousand Oaks, CA: Sage.

Kena, G., Aud, S., Johnson, F., Wang, X., Zhang, J., Rathbun, A., Wilkinson-Flicker, S., & Kristapovich, P. (2014). *The condition of education 2014* (NCES 2014-083). U.S. Department of Education, National Center for Education Statistics. Washington, DC. Available at http://nces.ed.gov/pubsearch.

Kena, G., Musu-Gillette, L., Robinson, J., Wang, X., Rathbun, A., Zhang, J., & Velez, E. D. V. (2015). *The condition of education 2015* (NCES 2015-144). National Center for Education Statistics. Washington, DC. Available at http://nces.ed.gov/pubsearch.

Kezar, A. J., Walpole, M., & Perna, L. W. (2015). Engaging low-income students. In S. J. Quaye & S. R. Harper (Eds.), *Student engagement in higher education: Theoretical perspectives and practical approaches for diverse populations* (pp. 237–255). New York, NY: Routledge.

Kim, D. H., & Schneider, B. (2005). Social capital in action: Alignment of parental support in adolescents' transition to postsecondary education. *Social Forces, 84*(2), 1181–1206.

Kincheloe, J. L. (2007). Critical pedagogy in the twenty-first century: Evolution for survival. In P. McLaren & J. L. Kincheloe (Eds.), *Critical pedagogy: Where are we now?* (pp. 9–42). New York, NY: Peter Lang.

Kincheloe, J. L (2008). *Knowledge and critical pedagogy: An introduction*. New York, NY: Peter Lang.

Kirst, M. W., & Bracco, K. R. (2004). Bridging the great divide: How the K–12 and postsecondary split hurts students, and what can be done about it. In M. W.

Kirst & A. Venezia (Eds.), *From high school to college: Improving opportunities for success in postsecondary education* (pp. 1–30). San Francisco, CA: Jossey-Bass.

Kirst, M., & Venezia, A. (2004). *From high school to college: Improving opportunities for success.* San Francisco, CA: Jossey-Bass.

Kisker, C. B. (2007). Creating and sustaining community college–university transfer partnerships. *Community College Review, 34*(4), 282–301.

Kleinfeld, J. (1975). Effective teachers of Eskimo and Indian students. *School Review, 83,* 301–344.

Klopfenstein, K., & Thomas, M. K. (2009). The link between Advanced Placement experience and early college success. *Southern Economic Journal, 75*(3), 873–891.

Koffman, D., & Tienda, M. (2008, March). *Missing in application: The Texas top 10% law and campus socioeconomic diversity.* Paper presented at American Educational Research Association Meeting, New York, NY. Available at www.researchgate.net/profile/Marta_Tienda/publication/254579047_Missing_in_Application_The_Texas_Top_10_Law_and_Campus_Socioeconomic_Diversity/links/541ae01d0cf2218008bfe7ce.pdf

Kram, K. E. (1985). *Mentoring at work: Developmental relationships in organizational life.* Glenview, IL: Scott, Foresman.

Krueger P. M., Tran, M. K., Hummer, R. A., & Chang, V. W. (2015). Mortality attributable to low levels of education in the United States. *PLoS ONE 10*(7): e0131809. doi:10.1371/journal.pone.0131809

Laden, B. V. (1999). Socializing and mentoring college students of color: The Puente project as an exemplary celebratory socialization model. *Peabody Journal of Education, 74*(2), 55–74.

Ladson-Billings, G. (1995). Toward a theory of culturally relevant pedagogy. *American Educational Research Journal, 32*(3), 465–491.

Ladson-Billings, G. (2006). From the achievement gap to the education debt: Understanding achievement in U.S. schools. *Educational Researcher, 35*(7), 3–12.

Lareau, A. (1994). Parent involvement in schooling: A dissenting view. In C. Fagano & B. Z. Werber (Eds.), *School, family, and community interaction: A view from the firing lines* (pp. 67–73). Boulder, CO: Westview Press.

Lareau, A. (2000). *Home advantage: Social class and parental intervention in elementary education.* Lanham, MD: Rowman and Littlefield.

Larson, R., Walker, K., & Pearce, N. (2005). A comparison of youth-driven and adult-driven youth programs: Balancing inputs from youth and adults. *Journal of Community Psychology, 33*(1), 57–74.

Lee, J., & Bowen, N. (2006). Parent involvement, cultural capital, and the achievement gap among elementary school children. *American Educational Research Journal, 43*(2), 193–218.

Lee, W. Y. (1999). Striving toward effective retention: The effect of race on mentoring African American students. *Peabody Journal of Education, 74*(2), 27–43.

Leiderman, S., Furco, A., Zapf, J., & Goss, M. (2000). *Building partnerships with college campuses: Community perspectives.* Washington, DC: The Consortium for the Advancement of Private Higher Education's Engaging Communities and Campuses Grant Program; The Council of Independent Colleges.

Lerner, R. M., Almerigi, J. B., Theokas, C., & Lerner, J. V. (2005). Positive youth development. *Journal of Early Adolescence, 25*(1), 10–16.

Levin, H. (2005, October). *The social costs of inadequate education.* Paper presented at Teachers College Symposium on Educational Equity. Teachers College, New York, NY. Available at https://www.tc.columbia.edu/centers/EquitySymposium/symposium/symposium.asp

Lin, N. (2000). Inequality in social capital. *Contemporary Sociology, 29*(6), 785–795.

Lindsay, L., & Justiz, M. (2001). *The quest for equity in higher education: Toward new paradigms in an evolving affirmative action era.* New York, NY: SUNY Press.

Long, M. C., Saenz, V., & Tienda, M. (2010). Policy transparency and college enrollment: Did the Texas top ten percent law broaden access to the public flagships? *The Annals of the American Academy of Political and Social Science, 627*(1), 82–105.

Lott, M. (2014, May 13). UCLA prof says stats prove school's admissions illegally favor Blacks. Available at www.foxnews.com/us/2014/05/13/ucla-prof-says-stats-prove-school-admissions-illegally-favor-blacks/

Lumina Foundation. (2015a). *The state of higher education in California: Blacks.* Los Angeles, CA: The Campaign for College Opportunity. Available at www.luminafoundation.org/files/resources/ca-state-of-higher-ed-blacks.pdf

Lumina Foundation. (2015b). *The state of higher education in California: Latinos.* Los Angeles, CA: The Campaign for College Opportunity. Available at www.luminafoundation.org/files/resources/state-of-higher-education-ca-2015.pdf

Lynch, M., Engle, J., & Cruz, J. L. (2010). Subprime opportunity: The unfulfilled promise of for profit colleges and universities. *The Education Trust.* Washington, DC.

Lynn, M., & Parker, L. (2006). Critical race studies in education: Examining a decade of research on US schools. *The Urban Review, 38*(4), 257–290.

MacKay, K. A., & Kuh, G. D. (1994). A comparison of student effort and educational gains of Caucasian and African-American students at predominantly White colleges and universities. *Journal of College Student Development, 35,* 217–223.

Maurrasse, D. J. (2002). *Beyond the campus: How colleges and universities form partnerships with their communities.* New York, NY: Routledge.

McDonough, P. (1997). *Choosing colleges: How social class and schools structure opportunity.* Albany, NY: SUNY Press.

McDonough, P. M. (2005). *Counseling and college counseling in America's high schools.* Alexandria, VA: National Association for College Admissions Counseling.

McKown, C., & Weinstein, R. S. (2008). Teacher expectations, classroom context, and the achievement gap. *Journal of School Psychology, 46*(3), 235–261.

MENTOR /National Mentoring Partnership. (2003) *Effective practice elements of effective practice* (2nd ed.). Alexandria, VA: Author.

MENTOR. (2013). *Elements of effective practice for mentoring* (3rd ed.). Washington, DC: Author. Available at www.mentoring.org/find_resources/elements_of_effective_practice/

Miller, D. B., & MacIntosh, R. (1999). Promoting resilience in urban African American adolescents: Racial socialization and identity as protective factors. *Social Work Research, 23*(3), 159–169.

Miller, P. M., & Hafner, M. M. (2008). Moving toward dialogical collaboration: A critical examination of a university-school-community partnership. *Educational Administration Quarterly, 44*(1), 66–110.

Milner, H. R. (2013). Analyzing poverty, learning, and teaching through a critical race theory lens. *Review of Research in Education, 37*(1), 1–53.

Milner, H. R. (2015). *Rac(e)ing to class: Confronting poverty and race in schools and classrooms.* Cambridge, MA: Harvard Educational Press.

Moore, C., & Shulock, N. (2010). *Divided we fail: Improving completion and closing racial gaps in California's community colleges.* Sacramento, CA: Institute for Higher Education Leadership, California State University. Available at www.edexcelencia.org/research/divided-we-fail-improving-completion-and-closing-racial-gaps-california-community-colleges

Morrow, K. V., & Styles, M. B. (1995). *Building relationships with youth in program settings: A study of Big Brothers Big Sisters.* Philadelphia, PA: Public/Private Ventures.

Museus, S. D., Ravello, J. N., & Vega, B. E. (2011). The campus racial culture: A critical race counterstory. In S. D. Museus & U. M. Jayakumar (Eds.), *Creating campus cultures: Fostering success among racially diverse student populations.* New York, NY: Routledge.

Myers, D., Olsen, R., Seftor, N., Young, J., & Tuttle, C. (2004). *The impacts of regular Upward Bound: Results from the third follow-up data collection.* MPR Reference No. 8464-600. Mathematica Policy Research. New York, NY: New York University Press.

Nagaoka, J., Roderick, M., & Coca, V. (2009). Barriers to college attainment: Lessons from Chicago. *Center for American Progress.* Washington, DC: Associated Press.

National Research Council and Institute of Medicine. (2013). *U.S. Health in International Perspective: Shorter Lives, Poorer Health.* Panel on Understanding Cross-National Health Differences Among High-Income Countries, S. H. Woolf & L. Aron (Eds.), Committee on Population, Division of Behavioral and Social Sciences and Education, and Board on Population Health and Public Health Practice, Institute of Medicine. Washington, DC: The National Academies Press.

Noguera, P. A. (1996). Confronting the urban in urban school reform. *The Urban Review, 28*(1), 11–19.

Noguera, P. A. (2001). Racial politics and the elusive quest for excellence and equity in education. *Education and Urban Society, 34*(1), 18–41.

Noguera, P. A. (2003). The trouble with Black boys: The role and influence of environmental and cultural factors on the academic performance of African American males. *Urban Education, 38*(4), 431–459.

Nord, C., Roey, S., Perkins, R., Lyons, M., Lemanski, N., Brown, J., & Schuknecht, J. (2011). *The nation's report card: America's high school graduates* (NCES 2011-462). U.S. Department of Education, National Center for Education Statistics. Washington, DC: U.S. Government Printing Office.

Oakes, J. (2003). *Critical conditions for equity and diversity in college access: Informing policy and monitoring results.* Los Angeles, CA: University of California Press.

Oakes, J. (2005). *Keeping track: How schools structure inequality.* New Haven, CT: Yale University Press.

Oakes, J., & Guiton, G. (1995). Matchmaking: The dynamics of high school tracking decisions. *American Educational Research Journal, 32*(1), 3–33.

Oakes, J., & Lipton, M. (2003). *Teaching to change the world.* New York, NY: McGraw-Hill.

Ogbu, J. U., & Wilson, J. (1990). *Mentoring minority youth: A framework.* East Lansing, MI: National Center for Research on Teacher Learning. (Premises ERIC Document Reproduction Service No. 354 293).

Orfield, G. (1996). The growth of segregation: African Americans, Latinos, and unequal education. In G. Orfield & S. E. Eaton (Eds.), *Dismantling desegregation: The quiet reversal of Brown v. Board of Education* (pp. 53–71). New York, NY: The New Press.

Orfield, G., Losen, D., Wald, J., & Swanson, C. B. (2002). Losing our future: How minority youth are being left behind by the graduation rate crisis. *Federal Register, 67*(231), 71–74.

Pampel, F. C., Krueger, P. M., & Denney, J. T. (2010). Socioeconomic disparities in health behaviors. *Annual Review of Sociology, 36,* 349–370.

Park, J. J., & Eagan, M. K. (2011). Who goes early? A multi-level analysis of enrollment via early action and early decision admissions. *Teachers College Record, 113*(11), 2345–2373.

Pascarella, E. T., & Terenzini, P. T. (1991). *How college affects students.* San Francisco, CA: Jossey-Bass.

President's Council of Advisors on Science and Technology (PCAST) (2010) Engage to excel: Producing one million additional college graduates with degrees in science technology, engineering, and mathematics.www.whitehouse.gov/ostp/pcast

President's Council of Advisors on Science and Technology (PCAST). (2012) Engage to excel: Producing one million additional college graduates with degrees in science technology, engineering, and mathematics. www.whitehouse.gov/ostp/pcast

Pearce, C. L. (2007). The future of leadership development: The importance of identity, multi-level approaches, self-leadership, physical fitness, shared leadership, networking, creativity, emotions, spirituality, and on-boarding processes. *Human Resource Management Review, 17*(4), 355–359.

Perna, L. W. (2002). Precollege outreach programs: Characteristics of programs serving historically underrepresented groups of students. *Journal of College Student Development, 43*(1), 64–83.

Perna, L. W. (2006). Studying college access and choice: A proposed conceptual model. In J. C. Smart (Ed.), *Higher education: Handbook of theory and research* (Vol. 21, pp. 99–157). Dordrecht, Netherlands: Springer.

Perna, L. W., Rowan-Kenyon, H. T., Thomas, S. L., Bell, A., Anderson, R., & Li, C. (2008). The role of college counseling in shaping college opportunity: Variations across high schools. *Review of Higher Education, 31*(2), 131–159.

Perna, L. W., & Titus, M. (2005). The relationship between parental involvement as social capital and college enrollment: An examination of racial/ethnic group differences. *Journal of Higher Education, 76*,(5) 485–518.

Person, A. E., & Rosenbaum, J. E. (2006). Chain enrollment and college enclaves: Benefits and drawbacks of Latino college students' enrollment decisions. *New Directions for Community Colleges, 2006*(133), 51–60.

Philip, K. (2000, August). Mentoring and young people. *The encyclopedia of informal education*. New York, NY: Infed.

Pitre, C. C., & Pitre, P. (2009). Increasing underrepresented high school students' college transitions and achievements: TRiO educational opportunity programs. *NASSP Bulletin.*

President's Council of Advisers on Science and Technology (PCAST). (2010). *Prepare and Inspire: K-12 education in science, technology, engineering, and math (STEM) for America's future.* [Report.] Washington, DC: The White House.

President's Council of Advisers on Science and Technology (PCAST). (2012). *Engage to excel: Producing one million additional college graduates with degrees in science, technology, engineering, and mathematics.* Washington, DC: The White House.

Prinstein, M. J., & Dodge, K. A. (2008). *Understanding peer influence in children and adolescents.* New York, NY: Guilford Press.

Quaye, S. J., Griffin, K. A., & Museus, S. D. (2015). Engaging students of colors. In S. J. Quaye & S. R. Harper (Eds.), *Student engagement in higher education: Theoretical perspectives and practical approaches for diverse populations* (pp. 15–36) New York, NY: Routledge.

Quigley, D. D. (2000). *Parents and teachers working together to improve third-grade achievement: Parents as learning partners (PLP) findings.* Los Angeles, CA: Los Angeles Compact on Evaluation, National Center for Research on Evaluation, Standards, and Student Testing/University of California, Los Angeles.

Quigley, D. D. (2002). *The Early Academic Outreach Program (EAOP) and its impact on high school students' completion of the University of California's preparatory coursework.* CSE Technical Report. Oakland, CA: Office of the President.

Research Alliance for New York City Schools. (2014). *New York City goes to college: A first look at patterns of college enrollment, persistence, and degree attainment for NYC high school students*. New York, NY: NYU Research Alliance for New York City Schools. Available at steinhardt.nyu.edu/scmsAdmin/media/users/sg158/PDFs/NYCGTC/Coca_NewYorkCityGoestoCollege_AFirstLook_Nov2014.pdf

Reynolds, R. (2010). "They think you're lazy," and other messages Black parents send their Black sons: An exploration of critical race theory in the examination of educational outcomes for Black males. *Journal of African American Males in Education, 1*(2), 143–165.

Reynolds, R. (2014). From their perspectives: Using critical race theory as a theoretical framework and methodology to examine the experiences of Black middle class parents in public secondary schools. In A. Dixson (Ed.), *Researching race in education: Policy, practice, and ethnography* (pp. 135–154). Charlotte, NC: Information Age.

Rhodes, B. A. (1971). *UCLA High Potential Program, 1968–1969*. Los Angeles, CA: University of California, Los Angeles.

Rhodes, J., & DuBois, D. (2007). Mentoring relationships and programs for youth. *Association for Psychological Science, 4*(17), 254–258.

Rhodes, J., & Lowe, S. (2008). Natural mentors and adolescent resiliency: A study with urban youth. *Child Care in Practice, 14*(1), 9–17.

Rhodes, J. E. (2002). *Stand by me: Risks and rewards in youth mentoring*. Cambridge, MA: Harvard University Press.

Roderick, M., Coca, V., & Nagaoka, J. (2011). Potholes on the road to college high school effects in shaping urban students' participation in college application, four-year college enrollment, and college match. *Sociology of Education, 84*(3), 178-211.

Rowan-Kenyon, H. T., Bell, A. D., & Perna, L. W. (2008). Contextual influences on parental involvement in college going: Variations by socioeconomic class. *The Journal of Higher Education, 79(5)*, 564–586.

Schimel, J., Arndt, J., Banko, K. M., & Cook, A. (2004). Not all self-affirmations were created equal: The cognitive and social benefits of affirming the intrinsic (vs. extrinsic) self. *Social Cognition, 22*, 75–99.

Schneider, B., & Stevenson, D. (1999). The ambitious generation. *Educational Leadership, 57*(4), 22–25.

Seftor, N. S., Mamun, A., & Schirm, A. (2009). *The impacts of regular Upward Bound on postsecondary outcomes 7–9 years after scheduled high school graduation*. Washington, DC: U.S. Department of Education, Policy and Program Studies Service.

Sellers, R. M., Chavous, T. M., & Cooke, D. Y. (1998). Racial ideology and racial centrality as predictors of African American college students' academic performance. *Journal of Black Psychology, 24*(1), 8–27.

Shapiro, D., Dundar, A., Yuan, X., Harrell, A., Wild, J., & Ziskin, M. (2014). *Some college, no degree: A national view of students with some college enrollment, but no completion (Signature Report No. 7)*. Herndon, VA: National Student Clearinghouse Research Center. Available at nscresearchcenter.org/signaturereport7/#Sig7-Discussion-2

Sipe, C. L. (1998). Mentoring adolescents: What have we learned? In J. B. Grossman (Ed.), *Contemporary issues in mentoring* (pp. 24–47). Philadelphia, PA: Public/Private Ventures.

Solórzano D., Ceja, M., & Yosso, T. (2000). Critical race theory, racial microaggressions, and campus racial climate: The experiences of African American college students. *The Journal of Negro Education, 69*(1/2), 60–73. Available at www.jstor.org/stable/2696265

Spring, J. (2010). *Deculturalization and the struggle for equality* (6th ed.) New York, NY: McGraw-Hill.

St. John, E. P., & Noell, J. (1989). The effects of student financial aid on access to higher education: An analysis of progress with special consideration of minority enrollment. *Research in Higher Education, 30*(6), 563–581.

Stanton-Salazar, R. D. (2001). *Manufacturing hope and despair: The school and kin support networks of US-Mexican youth*. New York, NY: Teachers College Press.

Stanton-Salazar, R. D., & Dornbusch, S. M. (1995). Social capital and the reproduction of inequality: Information networks among Mexican-origin high school students. *Sociology of Education, 68*, 116–135.

Steele, C. M. (1997). A threat in the air: How stereotypes shape intellectual identity and performance. *American Psychologist, 52*(6), 613–629.

Steele, C. M. (1998). Stereotyping and its threat are real. *American Psychologist, 53*, 680–681.

Steele, C. M., & Aronson, J. (1995). Stereotype threat and the intellectual test performance of African-Americans. *Journal of Personality and Social Psychology, 69*(5), 797–811.

Steele, C. M., Spencer, S. J., & Aronson, J. (2002). Contending with group image: The psychology of stereotype and social identity threat. *Advances in Experimental Social Psychology, 34*, 379–440.

Strayhorn, T. L. (2010). When race and gender collide: Social and cultural capital's influence on the academic achievement of African American and Latino males. *The Review of Higher Education, 33*(3), 307–332.

Swail, W. S. (2000). Preparing America's disadvantaged for college: Programs that increase college opportunity. *New Directions for Institutional Research, 2000*(107), 85–101.

Swail, W. S., & Perna, L. W. (2002). Pre-college outreach programs: A national perspective. In W. G. Tierney & L. S. Hagedorn (Eds.), *Increasing access to college: Extending possibilities for all students* (pp. 15–34). Albany, NY: State University of New York Press.

Swail, W. S., Redd, K. E., & Perna, L. W. (2003). *Retaining minority students in higher education: A framework for success. ASHE-ERIC Higher Education Report Volume 30* (2). San Francisco, CA: Jossey-Bass.

Swail, W. S., Quinn, K., Landis, K., & Fung, M. (2012). *A blueprint for success: Case studies of successful pre-college outreach programs.* Washington, DC: Educational Policy Institute. Available at www.educationalpolicy.org/publications/pubpdf/TG_CASESTUDY.pdf

Teranishi, R., Allen, W., &, Solórzano D. (2004). Opportunity at a crossroads: Racial inequality, school segregation, and higher education in California. *Teachers College Record, 106*(11), 2224–2245.

Terry, C. L., Sr., Flennaugh, T., Blackmon, S., & Howard, T. C. (2014). Does the Negro still need separate schools? Single-sex educational settings as critical race counterspace. *Journal of Urban Education, 49*(6), 666–697.

Texas Higher Education Coordinating Board. (2015). *Texas public higher education almanac: A profile of state and institutional performance and characteristics.* Austin, TX: Texas Higher Education Coordinating Board. Available at www.thecb.state.tx.us/download.cfm?downloadfile=A547D-FC2-A696-448C-751FCF9F23BE20FA&typename=dmFile&fieldname=filename

Tierney, W. G. (2000). Power, identity, and the dilemma of college student departure. In J. M. Braxton (Ed.), *Reworking the student departure puzzle* (pp. 1–25). Nashville, TN: Vanderbilt University Press.

Tierney, W. G. (2009). *Urban high school students and the challenge of access: Many routes, difficult paths.* New York, NY: Peter Lang.

Tierney, W. G., & Auerbach, S. (2005). Toward developing an untapped resource: The role of families in college preparation. In W. Tierney, Z. B. Corwin, & J. E. Colyar (Eds.), *Preparing for college: Nine elements of effective outreach* (pp. 29–48) Albany, NY: State University of New York Press.

Tierney, W. G., Bailey, T., Constantine, J., Finkelstein, N., & Hurd, N. F. (2009). *Helping students navigate the path to college: What high schools can do.* (NCEE #2009-4066). Washington, DC: National Center for Education Evaluation and Regional Assistance, Institute of Education Sciences, U.S. Department of Education. Available at ies.ed.gov/ncee/wwc/pdf/practice_guides/higher_ed_pg_091509.pdf

Tierney, W. G., & Hagedorn, L. S. (2002). *Increasing access to college: Extending possibilities for all students.* Albany, NY: SUNY Press.

Tierney, W. G., & Jun, A. (2001). A university helps prepare low income youths for college: Tracking school success. *Journal of Higher Education, 72*(2), 205–225.

Tinto, V. (1975). Dropout from higher education: A theoretical synthesis of recent research. *Review of Educational Research, 45*(1), 89–125.

Tinto, V. (1987). *Leaving college: Rethinking the causes and cures of student attrition.* Chicago, IL: University of Chicago Press.

Tinto, V. (1993). *Leaving college: Rethinking the causes and cures of student attrition* (2nd ed.). Chicago, IL: University of Chicago Press.

Torres, V. (2004). Familial influences on the identity development of Latino first year students. *Journal of College Student Development, 45*(4), 457–469.

Townsend, T., & Lanphier, E. (2007). Family influences on racial identity among African American youth. *Journal of Black Psychology, 33*(3), 278–298.

Treschan, L., & Mehrotra, A. (2012). *Unintended impacts: Fewer Black and Latino freshmen at CUNY senior colleges after the recession.* New York, NY: Community Service Society. Available at b.3cdn.net/nycss/2e01feab246663d4a8_lhm6b94lq.pdf

Tunstall, J. (2011). *Moving from critical consciousness to critical action: A phenomenological study of high school students' experiences in a social justice college access program.* Unpublished dissertation. University of California, Los Angeles.

Turner, C. S., Myers, S. L., & Creswell, J. W. (1999). Exploring underrepresentation: The case of faculty of color in the Midwest. *Journal of Higher Education, 70*(1), 27–59.

UCLA Community Programs Office. (2016). *Students heightening performance through education.* Available at http://www.uclacommunityprograms.org/sioc/students-heightening-academic-performance-through-education/

UCLA Early Academic Outreach Program. (2007, March). *EAOP news.* Available at www.eaop.ucla.edu/newsletter/Publication0607.pdf

University of California Office of the President. (2014). *University of California application, admission and enrollment of California resident freshmen for fall 1995 through 2014.* Oakland, CA: University of California Office of the President. Available at http://www.ucop.edu/institutional-research-academic-planning/_files/factsheets/2014/flow-frosh-ca-14.pdf

U.S. Bureau of Labor Statistics. (2015a). *Earnings and unemployment rates by educational attainment.* Washington, DC: U.S. Department of Labor. Available at www.bls.gov/emp/ep_chart_001.htm

U.S. Bureau of Labor Statistics. (2015b). Employment status of the civilian noninstitutional population 25 years and over by educational attainment, sex, race, and Hispanic or Latino ethnicity. Washington, DC: U.S. Department of Labor. Available at www.bls.gov/cps/cpsaat07.htm

U.S. Census Bureau. (1990). *Educational attainment.* Washington, DC: U.S. Department of Commerce: Available at www.census.gov/site-maintenance.html

U.S. Census Bureau. (2000). *Educational attainment 2000.* Washington, DC: U.S. Department of Commerce: Available at www.census.gov/prod/2003pubs/c2k-br-24.pdf

U.S. Census Bureau. (2010). *Educational attainment in the U.S.: 2010.* Washington, DC: U.S. Department of Commerce: Available at www.census.gov/hhes/socdemo/education/data/cps/2010/tables.html

U.S. Census Bureau. (2013). *Educational attainment in the United States: 2013 detailed tables.* Washington, DC: U.S. Department of Commerce: Available at http://www.census.gov/hhes/socdemo/education/data/cps/2013/tables.html

U.S. Department of Education. (2012a). National Center for Education Statistics. Public elementary and secondary school student enrollment and staff counts from the Common Core of Data: School Year 2010–2011. Washington, DC: U.S. Department of Education, National Center for Education Statistics. Available at https://nces.ed.gov/pubsearch/pubsinfo.asp?pubid=2013441

U.S. Department of Education. (2012b). *Percentage of first-time full-time bachelor's degree-seeking students at 4-year institutions who completed a bachelor's degree, by race/ethnicity, time to completion, sex, and control of institution: Selected cohort entry years, 1996 through 2005.* Washington, DC: U.S. Department of Education, National Center for Education Statistics. Available at nces.ed.gov/programs/digest/d12/tables/dt12_376.asp

U.S. Census Bureau. (2014a). *Income and poverty in the United States: 2013.* Washington, DC: U.S. Department of Commerce. Available at www.census.gov/content/dam/Census/library/publications/2014/demo/p60-249.pdf

U.S. Department of Education. (2014b). Projections of education statistics to 2022. Washington, DC: U.S. Department of Education, National Center for Education Statistics. Available at nces.ed.gov/pubs2014/2014051.pdf

U.S. Department of Education. (2015). Available at studentaid.ed.gov/repay-loans/default#consequences

U.S. Department of Education, National Center for Education Statistics. (2014). Table 326.10: Graduation rate from first institution attended for first-time, full-time bachelor's degree-seeking students at 4-year postsecondary institutions, by race/ethnicity, time to completion, sex, control of institution, and acceptance rate: Selected cohort entry years, 1996 through 2007. In U.S. Department of Education, National Center for Education Statistics (Ed.), *Digest of Education Statistics* (2014 ed.). Available at https://nces.ed.gov/programs/digest/d14/tables/dt14_326.10.asp.

U.S. Department of Education Office for Civil Rights. (2014). *Civil rights data collection: Data snapshot (school discipline).* Washington, DC: U.S. Department of Education Office for Civil Rights. Available at www.ocrdata.gov

Valenzuela, A. (1999). *Subtractive schooling: U.S.-Mexican youth and the politics of caring.* New York, NY: State University of New York Press.

Valliani, N., Siqueiros, M., & Dow, A. (2013). *The state of Blacks in higher education in California: The persistent opportunity gap. The Campaign for College Oppor-*

tunity. Available at http://collegecampaign.org/wp-content/uploads/2014/07/State_of_Higher_Education_Black-1.pdf

Vedantam, S. (2013, January). *Elite colleges struggle to recruit smart, low-income kids*. National Public Radio. Available at www.npr.org/2013/01/09/168889785/elite-colleges-struggle-to-recruit-smart-low-income-kids

Venezia, A., & Kirst, M. W. (2005). Inequitable opportunities: How current education systems and policies undermine the chances for student persistence and success in college. *Educational Policy, 19*(2), 283–307.

Walker, V. S. (1996). *Their highest potential: An African American school community in the segregated South*. Chapel Hill, NC: University of North Carolina Press.

Ward, N. L. (2006). Improving equity and access for low-income and minority youth into institutions of higher education. *Urban Education, 41*(1), 50–70.

Watts, R. J., Griffith, D. M., & Abdul-Adil, J. (1998). Sociopolitical development as an antidote for oppression—theory and action. *American Journal of Community Psychology, 27*(2), 255–271.

Watts, R. J., Williams, N. C., & Jagers, R. J. (2003). Sociopolitical development. *American Journal of Community Psychology, 31*(1–2), 185–194.

Wilson-Ahlstrom, A., Ravindranath, N., Yohalem, N., & Tseng, V. (2010). *Pay it forward: Guidance for mentoring junior scholars*. Washington, DC: The Forum for Youth Investment. Available at wtgrantfoundation.org/File%20Library/Publications/Pay%20It%20Forward%20Mentoring%20Guide.pdf

Wimberly, G. L. (2002). *School relationships foster success for African American students: ACT policy report*. Iowa City, IA: ACT. Available at files.eric.ed.gov/fulltext/ED475196.pdf

Yancey, A. K., Siegel, J. M., & McDaniel, K. L. (2002). Role models, ethnic identity, and health risk behaviors in urban adolescents. *Archives of Pediatrics and Adolescent Medicine, 156*, (1) 55–61.

Yosso, T. (2005). Whose culture has capital? A critical race theory of community cultural wealth. *Race, Ethnicity, and Education, 8*(1), 69–91.

Zeldin, S. (2004). Preventing youth violence through the promotion of community engagement and membership. *Journal of Community Psychology, 32*(5), 623–641.

Zimmerman, E., & Woolf, S. H. (2014). *Understanding the relationship between education and health* [Discussion paper]. Washington, DC: Institute of Medicine. Available at www.iom.edu/understandingtherelationship

Index

About the Authors

Tyrone Howard is professor of education and associate dean in the Graduate School of Education and Information Studies at University of California, Los Angeles. His research focuses on to race, culture, equity, and the education of students in urban schools.

Jonli D. Tunstall currently serves as director of two programs as part of the Academic Advance Program (AAP) team at the University of California, Los Angeles: VIP Scholars Program and Freshmen and Transfer Summer Program. In her current role as a member of the senior leadership team in the AAP, Dr. Tunstall oversees several programs and initiatives that works with first-generation, low-income, underrepresented students. In her tenure at UCLA, she has served in a number of formal and informal positions that have contributed to the acceptance and graduation of underrepresented undergraduate students across the country.

Terry K. Flennaugh is an assistant professor of Race, Culture, and Equity in Education in the Department of Teacher Education and the coordinator of Urban Education Initiatives for the College of Education at Michigan State University. He is also a core faculty member in African American & African Studies at the Center for Gender in Global Context at MSU. Dr. Flennaugh's research is primarily concerned with urban education and the educational experiences of Black males. Specifically, his interests revolve around identity formation and the sense-making processes Black males undergo as they matriculate through primary and secondary schools in urban contexts across the United States. Dr. Flennaugh is an editorial board member for *Urban Education* and his extensive experience with college access and educational enrichment programs has allowed him to serve on a number of university and community-based committees tasked with improving and diversifying institutions of higher education.

Irene Atkins was born in Trenton, New Jersey, and has a wide range of unique life experiences. After being recruited and participating as a student to the VIP Scholars program, she became passionate about social and educational change, and has dedicated her life to these causes since. After graduating from UCLA magna cum laude in 3 years, she is currently a graduate student in education policy at the University of Pennsylvania. While juggling classes at Penn, Irene also served as an 11th-grade teacher in West Philadelphia. Additionally, she facilitated a series of mindfulness courses for people of color in the Philadelphia community. Irene is passionate about her work and has recently launched her own independent practice that specializes in providing individual consultation and wellness solutions to education professionals. Her educational philosophies reflect her belief in the power of dialogue and student-centered education as a potent healing force.

Bree Blades is a native of Pasadena, California, and served as a VIP Scholars student, mentor, co-instructor, and undergraduate research fellow. She currently works with Gaining Early Awareness and Readiness for Undergraduate Programs (GEAR UP) at California State University, Monterey Bay, as the program coordinator for the Seaside/Salinas grant. Bree received her bachelor's degree in African American studies with a minor in education from UCLA and a master's degree in curriculum and instruction from Loyola University Chicago. Bree's passion for educational equity for underrepresented and underserved students has sparked her interest to pursue a career in enrollment management.

Jon Carroll is an emerging scholar who seeks to document the experience of students and teachers of color within the current educational landscape. He is currently a middle school dean at Harvard-Westlake School in Los Angeles, California. Dr. Carroll received his bachelor's from the University of Pennsylvania in 1999. He went on to earn a master's in education from Drexel University in 2006, and completed his PhD at the University of California, Los Angeles, in 2011. He has served as an adjunct professor in teacher education at Occidental College and is a frequent lecturer at UCLA.

Whitney Gouche is a native of Inglewood, California, who graduated from the University of California, Los Angeles, with her BA in sociology and African American studies in 2012. While at UCLA, Whitney served as a mentor and summer program coordinator for the VIP Scholars program. She recently graduated from the University of Pennsylvania with a master's degree in higher education. While studying at Penn she primarily focused on issues concerning race, gender, class, and inequality within education. Whitney's passion for social justice in education led her to a career in college access. She currently works as an academic program manager for EMERGE-HISD, a college access program dedicated to serving high-achieving, underserved students in the Houston Independent School District.

Tr'Vel Lyons is a master's student at the Harvard Graduate School of Education. A New Orleans native, Tr'Vel graduated from UCLA with a bachelor of art in philosophy from the University of California, Los Angeles, in 2014. After graduation he moved to Cordoba, Spain, and traveled extensively. He is a former student and academic mentor for the VIP Scholars program and worked as a lead researcher for UCLA's Black Male Institute.

Jerry Morrison II serves as the assistant director for the Vice Provost Initiative for Pre-College Scholars (VIPS) program at the University of California, Los Angeles (UCLA). In his role, he is responsible for supervising the efforts of 13 student mentors who service 10 high schools in the Los Angeles and Pasadena Unified School Districts. He also helps coordinate programming designed to empower and equip underserved high school students and parents with the tools needed to become competitively eligible for college admission. At the university level, Jerry has mentored and advised undergraduate students, helping them focus on successful retention and opportunities for graduate and professional school. Before coming to UCLA, Jerry received his bachelor's degree in political science with a minor in sociology from Loyola Marymount University. He then went on to earn a master's degree in post-secondary administration and student affairs from the University of Southern California. His previous experience in higher education stems from a background in admissions at LMU as well as academic advising at the university level.

Justyn K. Patterson is a 17-year student affairs professional at the University of California, Los Angeles. After earning his bachelor's degree in economics in 1998 from UCLA, he accepted a position at the university that would allow him to work on diversity and access issues in higher education. He joined the UCLA Early Academic Outreach Program (EAOP) where he served as a school site coordinator and academic programs coordinator until 2007. He left UCLA in 2007 to pursue an opportunity with the Los Angeles Urban League as the academic programs manager. After a year with the Urban League, Dr. Patterson returned to UCLA to assume the role of assistant director with EAOP. In 2012, he earned his doctorate of education at UCLA. His mixed-methods study illuminates the ways in which Black students interact with their sociocultural and institutional environments to earn admission to a selective university. His research challenges schools to develop a culture of care that supports achievement for all students in order to increase their educational resilience. Dr. Patterson is currently associate director of UCLA

BruinCorps—a program committed to serving more than 3,000 low-performing elementary and middle school students in underresourced communities throughout southern California by providing them with tutoring services and establishing local college centers. He also maintains his role as assistant director with the Early Academic Outreach Program.

Michelle Smith is currently a doctoral candidate in the Urban Schooling Division within UCLA's Graduate School of Education and Information Studies. She served as a teaching assistant for UCLA's VIP Scholars program for three summers in addition to her role as a graduate student researcher. With 10 years' experience as an educator in various capacities, Michelle's research interests include the matriculation of historically underrepresented students into postsecondary institutions, college readiness and the college choice process, and factors influencing STEM circuit preparation. In addition, Michelle is interested in local and school-level policies and practices that impact students' persistence within the P–20 pipeline as well as the role of outreach and access programs.

Ashley V. Williams is a graduate of the University of California, Los Angeles, with a bachelor's of arts degree in Afro-American studies and a minor in education. At UCLA she earned departmental honors as well as the Chancellor's Service Award. While at UCLA, Ashley was involved in several initiatives to increase the involvement of the university in providing educational services to surrounding Los Angeles communities. As a former student of the first cohort in the VIP Scholars program, Ashley continued her involvement with the program by working as a summer and academic mentor, and eventually, summer coordinator. Moreover, Ashley cofounded the Belizean-American Academic Mentors nonprofit organization where she works to connect Belizean-American professionals with current high school students in Belize. She spent a semester on site in Belize researching effective communication strategies with the minister of education and teaching English language and literature. Since graduating from UCLA, Ashley has served as a teacher-fellow for the Urban Prep Charter Academy for Young Men in Chicago, Illinois, where she developed curriculum and provided academic counseling to a cohort of all Black male freshman students. Currently, she is a master's candidate at the University of Illinois at Chicago (UIC), in the Youth Development program, where she is writing her thesis on Black youth expression through hip-hop in Chicago. Also, as a graduate assistant for the Office of Recruitment and Student Success in the College of Education at UIC, Ashley works closely with administration to develop culturally relevant programming and platforms for student advocacy.